G000143906

Circular Walks on the
Offa's Dyke Path
Volume 1—Prestatyn to Welshpool

Offa's Dyke Path near Waen Aberwheeler

Circular Walks on the
Offa's Dyke Path
Volume 1—Prestatyn to Welshpool

Jeff Lomax

Mara Publications

First published in March 1999 by Mara Publications, 22 Crosland Terrace, Helsby, Warrington, Cheshire, WA6 9LY.

All enquiries regarding sales telephone: (01928) 723744

ISBN 1 902512 01 4

To my wife Marion, a fellow Rambler

Text, maps and photographs © Jeff Lomax 1999
Cover photography and photographs on pages 2, 35, 46, 70 and 81 © Carl Rogers 1999

Cover photograph: Chirk Castle from Bronygarth
Back cover: Offa's Dyke Path near Waen Aberwheeler

All rights reserved. This publication must not be reproduced in any form without prior written permission from the publisher.

British Library Cataloguing-in-publication data.

A catalogue is available for this book from the British Library.

Whilst every effort has been made to ensure that the information in this book is correct, the author or the publisher can accept no responsibility for errors, loss or injury however caused.

Sketch maps based on the Ordnance Survey map with the permission of The Controller of Her Majesty's Stationery Office, Crown Copyright MC 87762M.

Printed and bound by Manchester Free Press telephone: 0161 864 4540

Contents

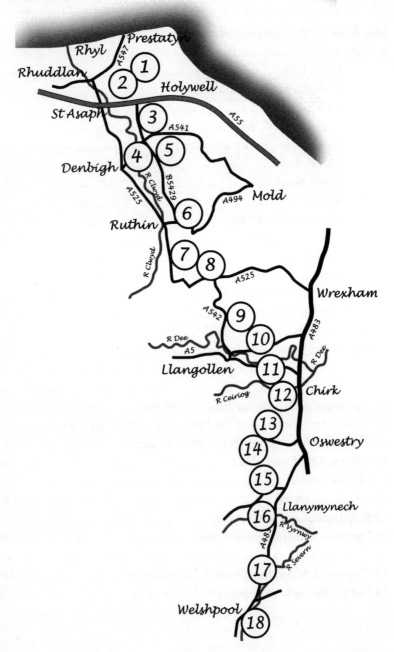

Introduction

THIS book contains 18 walks with as much variation as the countryside in which they are set. In length they range from 3¼ miles up to 9¼ miles, although most of the longer ones can be split or shortened. In other cases two walks can be combined into one. The walks cover about half of the 72 miles of the Offa's Dyke Path south from Prestatyn to a point level with Welshpool.

The history of man in the area goes back to the Bronze Age, when the Clwydian Hills provided a convenient route for a trackway—the motorway of the day—above the marshy river valleys. More obvious signs of man's occupation are the many hill forts—again particularly in the Clwydian Range, where nearly every hill is crowned with earthworks which are still impressive.

When the Romans arrived in the 1st century AD they found the area occupied by Celtic tribes. According to Ptolemy, the Deceangli occupied the area north of the River Dee but little seems to have been discovered of their way of life from excavation of the forts. It is considered that the culture of these western hill forts was not advanced. Mixed agricultural estates were worked by slaves or serfs, supporting small classes of cattle-raising freemen and their chiefs. South of the Dee the pre-Roman tribe was the Ordovici.

The Romans conquered Wales (as just about everywhere else), but after they left, the Welsh had a period without invasion (except from the sea, by Christian missionaries and less peaceful would-be immigrants from Ireland). The Anglo-Saxons did, however, sever the Welsh from their fellow Celts in Devon and Cornwall and in Cumbria, which led to the separate development of the Welsh and their language. In spite of sparring between the Anglo-Saxon kingdoms, the Welsh were steadily pressed back to the hilly regions. Offa became king of Mercia (southern England) in 757 and he decided to define his western boundary (and the eastern boundary of Wales) by building the dyke which bears his name.

Edward I was the first English king to conquer Wales, and most of the magnificent fortresses which he built still remain. Apart from the rebellion of Owain Glyndwr from 1400 to 1410 the Welsh have never felt free since then, but with the creation of a Welsh Assembly who knows what the future may hold?

Offa's Dyke

Research has shown that Offa's Dyke was built for over half the boundary between Mercia and Wales. It is believed that Offa himself decided on the line of the dyke, and this was done very skilfully, mostly making use of west-facing slopes to give good lines of sight, even though the dyke was not generally built to be defended.

Offa's Dyke near Selattyn

In size the dyke varies from a small bank, or even just a ledge on a steep slope, to a bank of up to 12 feet high with a ditch of similar size on the west. The variations are held to be caused by different "construction crews" as well as variations in terrain.

Apart from alleged traces on Walk 1, in the area covered by these walks, the Dyke is not met until south of the River Dee, as the fragments still remaining are mostly in industrial areas, and it was felt that a line over the Clwydian Hills would be preferable. (It is difficult to disagree with this!)

South of the Dee, walks 11 to 15 and 18 all include sections of the Dyke, with the finest example being on Walk 13, near Selattyn.

The Offa's Dyke Path

The enabling legislation for the creation of national long distance walking routes was the National Parks and Access to the Countryside Act of 1949. Although the idea of a route to follow the line of Offa's Dyke was accepted in 1949, the line was approved only in 1955, and it was not until July 1971 that it was opened. There was much delay in deciding the route and then there were lengthy negotiations with landowners and much work by local authorities in creating rights of way and in ensuring that they and the existing rights of way were passable, with good stiles and waymarking.

Two events boosted the process. The first was the transfer (in 1966) of responsibility for long distance paths from the National Parks Commission to the Countryside Commission, which had more powers. The rate of progress still did not satisfy everyone, and what is now the Offa's Dyke Association was set up in 1969 initially as a ginger group to push matters forward.

The Association is still very much in business and is the prime source of information about the Path and, indeed, about the

Welsh borders as a whole. They have an information centre in Knighton in association with a Heritage Centre, aptly adjacent to the site of the official opening of the path. For enquiries of any sort contact:- **The Offa's Dyke Association, West Street, Knighton, Powys LD7 1EW.**

The eventual line of the path is almost uniformly a delight. What is not uniform, though, is the form of that delight. Connoisseurs of almost any type of British scenery will find what they are looking for at some point on the walk, the only real exception being sea cliffs (but even here there are some pretty good imitations).

Geography

The north end of the Offa's Dyke Path (ODP) is in Prestatyn. It crosses the narrow coastal plain and then climbs onto low hills which give splendid views over the coast. Walks 1 and 2 are in this area, and can be combined.

The hills further south are higher, and beyond the gap which contains the A 55, can be regarded as the Clwydian Range. Although the hills are rounded ("Moels" rather than "Mynydds", rising only to 1820 feet) the range is like a miniature mountain range, and continues southwards for over 15 miles, with the fertile Vale of Clwyd accompanying it to the west. The ODP does not always run over the crest of the range, but when it does there are fine views to both east and west. From the highest points in clear weather the view eastward (over a mixed landscape including signs of limestone quarrying old and new and the Flintshire industrial belt) includes the estuaries of the Dee and Mersey, separated by the Wirral peninsula, with the haze of Merseyside in the distance. The more pleasant prospect westward over the Vale of Clwyd can include glimpses of Snowdonia. Walks 3 to 7 all involve climbs up onto the Range, if not all to high peaks. Walks 4 & 5 are another pair which can be combined.

Walk 8 is in farming land and can be linked with Walk 7. South of the Clwydian Range the land rises again, covered with a substantial forest, to a peat moorland. The underlying limestone outcrops spectacularly on the west and on the south, where it overlooks the Vale of Llangollen. Walks 9 & 10 (which could be linked by really strong walkers) are in this area.

The rivers Dee and Ceiriog flow eastwards to their junction. The wedge of pleasantly wooded farming land between them is crossed by Walks 11 & 12, which again can be linked. The next pair of walks, 13 & 14, is in even more pleasant country, well wooded and with streams cutting deep valleys between the hills, where a bulge of Shropshire, centred on Oswestry, protrudes into Wales.

Further south the hills, particularly at Llanymynech, have been quarried and mined for metal ores and limestone over many centuries, but the scars are being healed by nature and provide a fascinating study in regeneration. Walk 15 and the northern loop of Walk 16 are in this area.

The area for the rest of the walks is dominated by the wide flood plains of the rivers Vyrnwy and Severn, which meet over to the east of the route. When met the Vyrnwy is flowing east, but the Severn, about 35 miles from its source on Plynlimon, is flowing north before it turns first east to Shrewsbury and Ironbridge and finally south to Worcester, Gloucester and, as a widening estuary, past Bristol to Bridgwater Bay. The significant hills here are on the east of the river, including the Breidden Hills, with the only volcanic rock near these walks.

Walk Descriptions

The walk descriptions start with information on how to get to the start of the walk, by car or public transport. The main descriptive part intersperses details of the walk itself with less essential, but, I hope, interesting snippets of general information and comments. The latter are *in italics*, so, if all you want to do is get the walk finished as soon as possible, ignore the bits in italics!

Public transport information

All walk descriptions include information on how to get to the start by bus, and, in a few cases, by train. Some services are very infrequent, and there are very few services which operate on Sundays. Since the chaos immediately after the deregulation of bus services the situation has largely settled down, but there are still liable to be changes, so it is advisable to make a last check shortly before using the service. Telephone numbers of operators mentioned are as follows:-

Operator	Telephone No.
Arriva Cymru	01745 343721
Bryn Melyn	01978 860701
George Edwards & Son	01978 757281
G H A Coaches	01978 753598
K D Coaches	01745 571200
M & H Coaches	01745 812057
Midland Red North (Oswestry)	01691 652402
Midland Red North (Shrewsbury)	01743 344028
Tanat Valley Coaches	01691 780212

If difficulties are met with (for instance if the operator changes), further information, usually including maps and timetables of services, can be obtained from local authorities, as follows:-

Denbighshire	01824 706968
Flintshire	01352 704035
Wrexham	01978 266166
Shropshire	0345 056785
Powys	01597 826643

Train information can be obtained from the national enquiry number, 0345 484950.

Even for those not using cars it would be possible to do a number of these walks while staying in the same place. For instance there are bus links from Ruthin for walks 6, 7, and 8.

Maps

There are sketch maps with each of the walk descriptions (at a scale of 1:25 000—about 2½ inches to the mile). However it is advised that walkers also have another map covering the whole area of the walk. The relevant ones are listed in the introductory parts of the description. This will enable walkers to work out the route on a map with more information, so that it will be more obvious if the route is departed from, and ways of getting back on route can be seen.

Precautions

Although these walks are not in wild country by any means, care should be taken. Boots are certainly necessary, as there is rough ground on each of the walks. Waterproofs and, particularly if height is being gained, extra layers of clothing are advisable and a compass could come in handy at times. In general it should not be necessary, but (for instance) if a mist comes down suddenly when on the higher hills, or if the route was lost, it could be very helpful in conjunction with a map. The only other thing to be advised (in particular if only one or two people are walking) is that someone else should know where people are walking and what time they should return, so that the emergency services can be informed if necessary.

Welsh

Rather than produce a glossary of useful terms, I have tried to translate place names etc. into English whenever I could. The translations are in brackets [] after the Welsh on its first appearance in a walk. I hope that readers may find this useful, but I am sure that I will have dropped some awful clangers. For the most part I have only worked from dictionaries, which is not easy because of the way in which initial letters of Welsh words can change into other letters according to complicated rules. I am slightly heartened by having found inconsistencies in translated names in works of reference! In case there is a subsequent issue of this book I should be grateful for any corrections, or translations of words or phrases I have not even attempted.

Errors & Problems

I apologise in advance for any discrepancies between my instructions and what is actually found on the ground. I hope that any such problems will be caused by changes since I wrote. I am afraid that these can happen with anything— trees, hedges, fences, even rights of way can be removed or added. Again I should be grateful to be told about necessary corrections, but problems with the rights of way should be reported to the relevant local authority. These are:-

Denbighshire: Access Officer (Rights of Way), Council Offices, Ruthin LL15 1AT

Flintshire: Head of Development Control, Highways/Transportation & Engineering Dept., County Hall, Mold CH7 6NF

Powys: Head of Countryside Access, Technical Services Dept., County Hall, Llandrindod Wells LD1 5LG

Shropshire: Head of Countryside Service, The Shire Hall, Abbey Foregate, Shrewsbury SY2 6NW

Wrexham: Highways and Transportation Services Manager, Crown Buildings, Wrexham LL11 1WQ

Acknowledgments

Firstly I should like to thank my wife Marion; not just for her general encouragement but also for being the first line for checking material and for doing the lettering on maps. My brother Bob Lomax has advised on the layout and Hilary Sieff has helped with Welsh translation.

The essential job of "proof walking" has been carried out by Phil Evans, Richard Evans, Jack and Joyce Fort, Bill Lomas and the Vale of Clwyd Group of Volunteers, Hazel Morgan, Bernard Raftery, Dafydd Roberts, Audrey, Carl and Jack Rogers and David Telfer.

I have received much helpful advice from fellow members of the Ramblers Association in the areas of the walks, in particular Rob Ayerst, Gwen Evans, Jack Fort, Cyril Jones, Val Jones, Bill Lomas and Carol Mason.

I am also extremely grateful for information and practical assistance from the local authorities of Denbighshire (Howard Sutcliffe and Adrian Walls), Flintshire (John Hill), Powys (Mark Chapman), Shropshire (David Morris and James Lanyon) and Wrexham (Susan Briscoe and Sarah Rogerson). Walkers everywhere owe an immense debt to devoted local authority officers, without whom no walks at all would be possible.

And finally ....

It has been great fun doing the walking and writing this book. I hope that the users of it also enjoy the walking in this wonderful countryside.

Jeff Lomax

Trelawnyd & Gwaenysgor

A gentle walk mostly through farmland, with historic villages and some fine views, particularly of the coast from the Great Orme to the Wirral.

Distance: *5 miles, with up to ½ mile further to the top of Gop Hill.*

Start: *Begin in Trelawnyd, which is on the A5151 two miles east of Dyserth. High Street, towards Llanasa, goes north beside the Memorial Hall. There is a small car park about 100 yards up it on the right. Grid ref: 091 798 (Landranger 116, Pathfinder 755 - 737 also needed for the walk).*

By bus: *Trelawnyd and Gwaenysgor are both served by the 32 service between Glan yr Afon and Prestatyn (K D Coaches/Arriva Cymru). Alight in Trelawnyd at the Memorial Hall, and walk up High Street past it.*

Trelawnyd ["Tre" means "town" and "lawnyd" probably relates to a personal name] has existed for a long time. Between 1700 and 1954 it was known as Newmarket. The oldest building is the church, which is seen at the end of the walk. It is reported to be over-restored and gloomy inside, but will probably be locked. There is a 13th century cross to the south in the churchyard, with Crucifixion scenes on it. Newmarket is mentioned on many of the headstones.

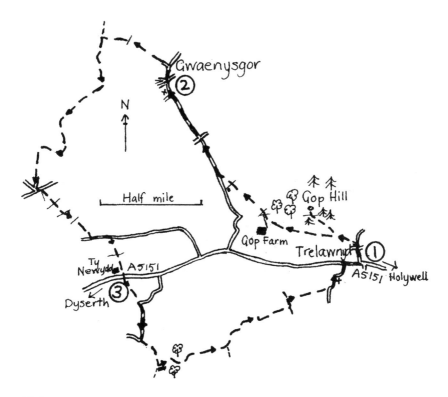

The Route

1. Go up High Street. Turn into a track on the left just past Bron Haul [Sunny Hillside]. Pass the new houses and proceed to a very elaborate stone stile. *To the south on a clear day the northern end of the Clwydian Hills can be seen.* Ahead the path enters a meadow rich in flowers, with butterflies attracted particularly by the marjoram.

If it is wished to visit the summit of Gop Hill, a permissive (but almost invisible) path on the right leads up, slanting to the left, to a kissing gate through the wall at the top of the meadow, at a gap in the conifers. The top of the hill is reached through a band of blackthorn, and is rich in lime-loving plants.

Relics of Stone Age man have been found in caves in the hill, which is crowned by an immense, probably Bronze Age, stone burial mound, the largest in Wales. From the top there is a splendid view. To the north can be seen the Tudor house Golden Grove. To the east is the mouth of the Dee, with Hilbre Island and the Wirral peninsula. Southwards, across the plain, lie the Clwydian Hills. Southwest is the prominent hill of Y Foel [The Hill], with quarrying nibbling at the fort of Moel Hiraddug ["Moel" is a rounded hill, and Hiraddug is either a person's name or means "long attack"]. Further round, the Great Orme limits the view of the coast, except on an extremely clear day, when Anglesey may be glimpsed beyond it. The most northerly traces of Offa's Dyke are supposed to be on Gop Hill but they are not obvious on the ground to the uninitiated.

Having feasted your eyes on the view return to the right of way. The path heads towards Gop Farm, but swings right to avoid it.

A small building outside the farm fence is a 17th century dovecote. Nesting niches can be glimpsed through the gap where the roof was. This is probably the columbarium in which bones from the caves on Gop Hill were stored temporarily in 1912.

Keep to the fence beyond the dovecote, and go over two stiles in quick succession. Head down the field towards a small electricity substation in the bottom left hand corner. *On the right, surrounded by trees, is the site of an old spring, Ffynnon Wen [White Spring].* The next field is entered by a gap or stile to the right of the building. Cross the next field to a stile in the left hand hedge. This leads to quite a busy road. Turn right here and go ahead at the crossroads to reach Gwaenysgor [Meadow by fortification].

A board on the green gives interesting information about the village. It has old houses, but much modern infilling. The church is apparently 12th century, and the roughly circular churchyard is also ancient.

Ancient cross in Trelawnyd churchyard

2. Keep to the right of the village stores. *(The Eagle and Child inn is down the lane to the left here.)* Take the next narrow lane to the left, just before a house bearing the date 1680. Proceed down the path past the modern bungalows. *Shortly on the left is the well which once supplied the whole village. Now it is firmly locked to prevent any use or misuse.* Continue down the path to a stile, and then up into an area of gorse. Another stile leads to the Offa's Dyke Path, waymarked with the acorn signs. Turn left here down through a blackthorn thicket.

The next section of path undulates along the edge of a hill as though along a cliff top. However, instead of the sea below, it is the coastal plain. Part of this is farmland, but just as much is taken up by the buildings of Rhyl [The Hill] (to the left) and Prestatyn [Village of Priests] (to the right), together with caravan sites, golf courses and playing fields. To the left the Great Orme may be seen, rising above the Little Orme and Colwyn [Puppy] Bay.

The path skirts an old quarry, passes through two kissing gates and descends to the private road to "Red Roofs". Turn left here, climbing past a disused quarry on the left to another metal kissing gate, which leads out onto a public road. *In spring there are white violets here.* Turn left for a few yards before climbing a stile on the right to leave the road.

The path is clear down through four fields to a road, but stiles are of the awkward local type, tall, narrow and with metal rungs. At the road turn left. Watch out for the stile on the right. (If footpaths are wet the next stretch can be avoided by continuing on the road to the A5151 and then turning right—see the map.) Over the stile head slightly to the left up the hill to reach a gate and stile in the hedgeline on the crest of the hill. *Gop Hill is quite close on the left, appearing to be half wooded.* Go down to a stile which is behind the slurry pit at the farm of Ty Newydd [New House]. The road here is the A5151, and turning left would take you back into Trelawnyd.

3. Cross the road and stile and keep to the left-hand fence to another stile. Turn right down the little road. The quarry on Y Foel is prominent to the right. When the road turns back to the right continue ahead. *(Walk 2 joins here)*. Pass the trout hatchery on the left and where the Offa's Dyke Path and Walk 2 turn right as a bridleway by a house with an arched gateway, take the other bridleway to the left.

The track soon enters a wood, with many sycamores with ivied trunks, and winds gently about with occasional glimpses of the stream on the left. *The main track turns left across the stream to a house, which is probably a lodge for Henfryn [Oldhill] Hall, which is behind the trees across the stream.* Our track continues ahead. After fording a shallow stream turn left at a junction of paths and cross the main stream by a bridge. A short muddy section is best avoided on the right. After that the track climbs in a tunnel of vegetation, with occasional views of Gop Hill to the left, its "pimple" of a cairn very prominent from this angle.

Turn left at another T-junction of paths and soon go right over a stile. Keep to the fence on the right in the first field to a stile and then go along the centre of the next field to a stone stile into a road. Turn left here and follow the road past the church. The road comes out onto the A5151. Turn right, with the Memorial Hall prominent ahead, to find the car park and bus stops.

Round Y Foel From Dyserth

This walk is a circumambulation of Y Foel, with an extension to the village of Cwm. On a clear day the views could hardly be bettered.

Distance: *5 miles.*

Start: *Start in Dyserth, on the A5151, near the Post Office (PO). There is a small car park off Rhodfa Thomas [Thomas Avenue], which goes off the A5151 towards Holywell from the PO. Grid ref. 058 790 (Landranger 116, Pathfinder 755).*

By bus: *Dyserth is well served by the 35 and 36 circular routes (Arriva Cymru), which also go to Rhyl, Prestatyn and Rhuddlan. Alight at Dyserth Post Office.*

Dyserth [A desert place, hermit's cell or church] is not an obviously attractive place, even though it was mentioned (as Dissard) in the Domesday Book in 1086. However, it has an attractive waterfall (with an entrance fee) and the church has parts from the 13th and 14th centuries, a Jesse window, possibly from Basingwerk Abbey, and an inscribed pillar in the churchyard. The waterfall and church are both along the B5119 to the north.

The Route

1. Start along the A5151 heading eastwards (towards Holywell). *Between the houses on the right are occasional glimpses of Y Foel [The*

Hill], which the walk will go round. After going down into a dip it is advisable to cross the road for a short distance when the footpath on the right stops. There is a waymark here for the North Wales path. Our route, however, soon goes off on the other side, along a path just before a fierce metal fence. Go over a stile beside a gate and keep left, with the fence on the left. Come out into a field, with another stile ahead, again beside a gate. Go over the stile. There is now a stream pleasantly gurgling down to the left. Go ahead on a more obvious path and through another gateway.

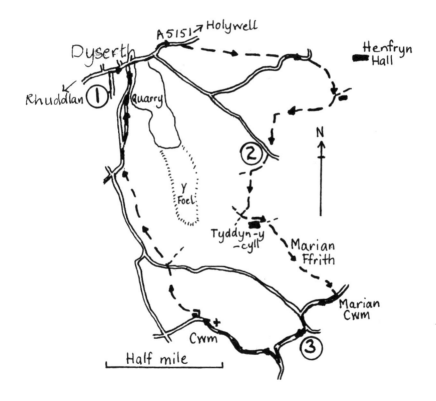

Y Foel is now on the right and it is obvious from a number of places that its right (north) end has been quarried away, leaving only a thin layer of rock on the outside (rather like a tooth which has been drilled out, but not filled). Quarrying goes back at least to the time of the battle of Hiraddug, between two pairs of brothers in 1034, with the iron ore haematite being worked there from a very early date. The ancient British hill fort of Hiraddug once covered the whole top of the hill.

The path goes along a shelf (along which it was once intended to run a railway), with the winding, pleasantly tree-lined stream down on the left, and slightly higher ground to the right. Eventually a stile leads out onto a lane near Pandy [Fulling Mill] Mill Farm (now renamed Grove Mill Cottage). Turn left, and follow the lane, passing the remains of Grove Mill.

At one time Marian [Holm] Mills (as it was then) had four mills and was a popular place for excursions from the coast. Grove Mill, the last to survive, milled corn and closed for the last time in 1924. Beyond it, to the right, are the remains of the leet which brought water to power the mill.

The route soon crosses the line of the leet, which went over the path from the pool which is now the Marian Mill Trout Hatchery. When the lane turns sharp left go ahead, joining the Offa's Dyke Path (ODP) and Walk 1. The waymark down the track points to Cwm (even though that is not on the ODP). Pass the trout hatchery, and turn right along a bridleway at a house with an archway unaesthetically supported by RSJs. *(Walk 1 turns left here.)*

The path is now enclosed, with a waterworks building on the left. Keep right where a lesser path goes to the left by the waterworks fence and go through two gates with stiles. Just before a third gate the path turns left over a stile and keeps along the fence on the left to another stile. From this there is an intermittent hawthorn hedge on the left. *When the hedge stops there is a good view of Henfryn [Oldhill] Hall back to the left across the valley, with Gop Hill behind (see Walk 1).* Continue ahead to a stile (one of the old-style ones with metal rungs and narrow for anyone with a large rucksack—or large anything else for that matter!). *As you climb the stile the sea can be seen to the right.*

2. The stile leads onto a road, and twenty yards or so to the left is a stone stile on the right. The stile leads to a stony track, which climbs towards Y Foel, but when the track bears right the ODP turns left over a stile and continues with the hedge on the right. Bear round to the right to a ladder stile and then bend right round the edge of a hummock to a stone slab stile. *(There is considerable variety of stiles on this walk, with some of the metal runged ones having had cross pieces added, which are a big improvement.)* Turn left along the farm track, passing to the left of Tyddyn-y-cyll [Hazel Trees Farm]. Continue along the track, but just after it bends left turn right over a stile. Go up the field to a stile to the left of the top right hand corner. *Looking back from here part of Prestatyn [Village of Priests] can be seen to the left of the hill of Graig Fawr [Great Rock].*

Bear left, away from the fence/wall/hedge on the right, up the hill to a clump of trees which prove to be growing from a small pit, probably once a small quarry. There is a guide post here, directing up to a small col near the top of Marian Ffrith [Holm Pasture].

All the way up this climb the view has been extending. On a clear day the mountains of Snowdonia can be picked out. To the left the coast extends to the Great Orme, but the northern end of Anglesey may be visible even beyond that.

From the col descend to Marian Cwm [Holm Valley], slanting left down the slope to a gate in line with a white house. Beyond the gate a road is soon reached. Leave the ODP here, turning right through the village. *Most of the newer property is named in English, the older in Welsh.* Turn left at the first junction (unless you want to turn right for a shorter way back) and right at the second (which should be signed to Cwm and Rhuallt).

3. Go down the hill, which increases in steepness, and winds with glorious views over the Vale of Clwyd. *To the right there was once a mine which produced nearly 30,000 tons of haematite in 15 years.* Turn right with the sign to Cwm and Rhuddlan at the next junction. Keep left between the 30 speed limit signs for the village of Cwm [Valley].

This is a very linear village. The church, which dates from the 12th century, is dedicated to two 6th century Celtic Saints, Mael and Sulien, and has some interesting contents, but is not normally open. There is an unusual double belfry. The village also has a public house, the Blue Lion Inn.

Pass the church and the pub and take a footpath on the right just before the next building on the right. Pass up the field, with

Blue Lion Inn, Cwm

a fence on the left, to a stile on the left. Go over this and continue to the top of the field, below the wood. Turn left, on a waymarked, stiled path. At the end of the wood continue ahead towards the largest tree (a sycamore) in a hedgeline ahead. *There are fine views up and down the Vale of Clwyd from here.* Follow the fence round to a stile. *Y Foel is very prominent ahead, and there is a good view back to Cwm.* Go over the stile, and keep the fenceline on the right on the descent to a wooden stile onto a road. Turn left for a few paces. *(This is the point which would have been reached by turning right after Marian Cwm, soon after passing a stone house on the right on the steep descent.)*

Go right up stone steps to a stile. From this take the path slanting left, more or less on the level, not the one climbing to the right. *A very built-up stretch of coastline, from Rhyl [The Hill] to Llandudno [Church of St Tudno], can be seen ahead and to the left.* The path is clear, past gorse, hawthorn and bracken, and then trees to the left which spoil the view. The path enters woodland and becomes more of a track, basically downhill. Soon the southward sprawl of Dyserth is below to the left, but the path is pleasant through the wood to a makeshift stile. This leads to a rough road which soon comes out onto a proper road, which is solid with houses. Soon Upper Foel [Hill] Road to the right gives a quieter option, with better views to Rhuddlan [Red Riverbank] and beyond. Shortly before the two roads merge again there are three limekilns to the right (two of them blocked up). Continue along the road to the A5151, and turn left to return to the start of the walk.

Tremeirchion

Pleasant fields and streams, then a climb of about 500 feet to an elevated section of the Offa's Dyke Path, with views of the Vale of Clwyd and beyond.

Distance: *4¼ miles.*

Start: *Tremeirchion [Hamlet of horses] is on the B5429 between Rhuallt and Bodfari [House of Mary]. The parish church (Corpus Christi) is up the road to Holywell. The road here, or further up, outside the Salusbury Arms, is wide enough for parking. Grid ref: 083 731 (Landranger 116, Pathfinder 755).*

By bus: *The only bus service of any possible use for walking from Tremeirchion is the 40 from Bodfari (Wednesday, Friday and Saturday only) (M & H Coaches). Alight at the main road junction (grid ref: 082 729), near an elaborate memorial seat bearing the apt quotation "I will lift up mine eyes unto the hills", and walk north along the B5429 to join the route.*

The history of Tremeirchion goes back a long way. Stone Age tools have been found in a cave nearby. The circular churchyard is ancient and parts of the church itself may be 14th century. There are interesting tombs. More recently the house Brynbella, south of the village, was built for Samuel Johnson's friend Mrs Thrale and her second husband, Gabriel Piozzi, a music teacher.

The Route

1. Go down the road past the church and turn through the kissing gate into the school playground. Before the school building turn left down a grass track and go over a stile, the step of which is a recycled direction arrow to Prestatyn. Go down the path between a sturdy stone wall and the remains of a hawthorn hedge. Across the top of a small quarry the wall is replaced by a metal fence. Beyond this the path descends to the B5429 road.

Turn right along the road, passing a road on the left and a farm on the right. At the junction with the next lane on the left take a stile into the field. Keep roughly parallel to the stream on the right to cross two sets of two stiles. Go rather to the right of the direction shown on the last of these to reach the next stile and gradually move closer to the stream until there is a stile in the hedge on the right. Go over this and the sturdy wooden bridge beyond.

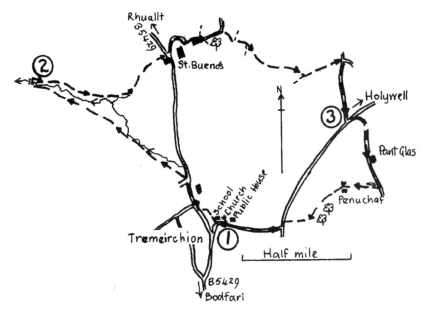

2. Turn right to go up the other side of the stream. Go through four fields, keeping close to the stream on the right.

The hill ahead is Moel Maenefa [Hill of Eva's Stone], and the prominent building below it is St Beuno's College, which was built in 1848 for the training of Jesuit priests, but is now a Retreat Centre. Gerard Manley Hopkins was there from 1874 to 1877, and the surrounding countryside inspired much of his finest poetry. St Beuno was a major Christian missionary long before the Normans. He was the uncle of St Winifred, and features in the legend of the founding of Holywell.

When there is no way ahead through to the next field turn left, with a hedge on the right until a waymark to the right shows the way through a gate. Continue up the field, initially with a hedge on the left, to reach a stile on the left of a house. The stile leads to the B5429 again.

There is a fine view back from the stile. On a clear day the mountains of Snowdonia may be seen across the Vale of Clwyd. In the Vale the squat tower of St Asaph Cathedral can be seen to the left of the spire of the white church at Bodelwyddan [Home of the Wood Spirit]. (Although often referred to as a marble church the main exterior material is magnesium limestone, but there are Belgian red marble and alabaster inside.) The coast can be seen from Rhyl [The Hill] to the Great Orme beyond Llandudno [Church of St Tudno]. An elevated section of the new A55 can be seen and, probably, its traffic heard.

Cross the B5429 to a minor road, which leads up past St Beuno's. The road continues to wind and climb. Pass paths to the left (the Offa's Dyke Path - ODP) and right. *The latter goes into a wood which is a favourite haunt of tits and other small birds.* When the road turns left go right on a bridleway, continuing to climb between fences. Ignore a path to the left. When the bridleway goes right bear left up to a stile.

The views over the Vale of Clwyd are now even more extensive. The River Clwyd [Hurdle] can be seen meandering as it approaches the sea beyond Rhuddlan [Red Riverbank] and Rhyl. It may be possible to see the NE corner of Anglesey beyond the Great Orme.

Continue up the hill between the gorse to another stile and then less steeply across grass to the next.

The main part of the Clwydian Range is half right ahead, the most prominent summit being Moel-y-Parc [Park Hill] with its transmitting mast. (See Walk 5.)

Bear right to a stile in the corner of the field beside a gate. Turn left along a track, climbing again. When the track reaches a road turn right along it, now downhill.

3. At a T-junction turn left and very soon right on another road, which bends to the right. Pass Pant Glas [Blue Valley] on the left and continue down into a dip. Just after a pool on the right turn right on the track leading to Penuchaf [Upper Head] (leaving the ODP). Go between the farm buildings and over a stile into the field. Bear left down to the right hand side of a small wood. Continue with this on the left, climbing a fence and going on to the next fence. Turn right here and keep the fence on the left, passing to the left of a large clump of gorse.

A stile leads to a set of steps leading down to a road. Turn left along this and turn right with it in about 100 yards to return to Tremeirchion. *Take care along the narrow, busy road. It is advisable to keep to the right of the road in single file.*

Waen Aberwheeler

After a moderate climb onto the Clwydian Range there is a level stretch with views across and beyond the Vale of Clwyd. The descent and return are through farming country.

Distance: *6 miles (5 miles with some road walking rather than fields at the end).*

Start: *Begin at the only real junction in Waen Aberwheeler, on the B5429 about ½ mile south of its junction with the A543. There is a small parking layby to the north of the junction, opposite the road Bro Llewenni. Grid ref: 097 694 (Landranger 116, Pathfinder 772).*

By bus: *Waen Aberwheeler is served by the 14 service between Denbigh and Mold (M & H Coaches).*

Waen [Meadow] Aberwheeler is presumably so called to distinguish it from two other Waens to north and south within three miles. Aberwheeler implies that it is where the River Wheeler (or Chwiler [Chrysalis or Pupa]) runs into the River Clwyd [Hurdle]. This is not quite accurate, as the confluence is a mile away. Strangely the village name on the road signs is given simply as Aberwheeler/Aberchwiler. The village has no shop or public house. There is a Welsh Calvinistic Presbyterian Chapel, which may still be in use, although it has nothing outside to attract visitors, such as service times.

The Route

1. Start up the road with a warning of a weak bridge two miles ahead, heading north-east from the junction with the B5429, soon passing Porth y Waen [Meadow Gate] on the right. Continue along the road, with the Clwydian Range looking imposing ahead. *(Do not worry, you will not be climbing far on this walk!)* Pass a farm (Efail y Waen [Meadow Smithy]) on the right, and then the driveway to The Grove Hall Home for Mental Disorders. *To the left, across the A541 can be seen the remains of an old quarry near Bodfari [House of Mary]. Nature is fighting back, and returning its beauty.* At the next road junction turn right with the Offa's Dyke Path (ODP) acorn waymark. Pass a house in red and yellow brick.

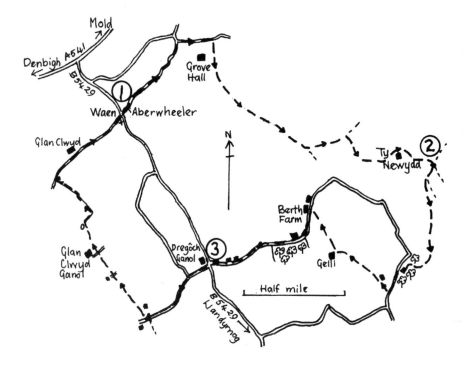

Turn right just before a post box in the wall (only collection 7.45 am!) and pass a house before turning left over a stile. Head across the field with the back of Grove Hall to the right. The way is obvious up over stiles which have no crosspieces but are easy for the longlegged. There is soon a good view back across to Bodfari, with its prominent church. From a better stile go up the hill on a clearer path.

Below to the right is Waen Aberwheeler, with Denbigh behind. [Denbigh may mean little hill, but there is a nice story that it originates from a dragon slayer shouting "Din Bych" —no dragon!].

Pass a marker post and bear slightly right. From the next stile the ODP takes a route along the bottom of bracken moor (a shoulder of Moel y Parc [Park Hill]), and then continues ahead when the fence turns to the right. Climb to a marker post and then turn right more on the level on a bridleway.

The white church at Bodelwyddan [Home of the Wood Spirit] can be seen to the northwest on a clear day (with a large hospital to its right), and Penycloddiau [Hill of trenches] is nearer ahead. (See Walk 5.)

Keep left on the bridleway when a clear track goes to the right, but turn right at the next two path junctions to cross a stream. After the farm (Ty Newydd [New House]) continue ahead rather than turning right and continue up, passing ruined farm buildings and going through a number of gates, to the col below Penycloddiau, linking briefly there with Walk 5.

2. Turn right over a stile with the ODP signs, but when they point left up the hill bear right, keeping a fence immediately on the right even when the main track bears left. Go through a gate and continue on a grassy track between bracken and gorse.

The farm below on the right is Bwlch [Pass] and the countryside below is well endowed with trees. The grassy track descends the slope gently and bends round to the right to cross a small valley and go up into a wood containing sycamore, mountain ash and silver birch. From the crest of a small ridge the path swings

Looking towards Bodfari on the Offa's Dyke Path

round to the left to a gate onto a small road. Turn right here and left very soon at a T-junction.

Soon turn right through the gate to Gelli Uchaf [Upper Grove]. Pass to the left of the cottage and continue with the remains of a hedge to the right. Go over the stile to the right of an oak tree in the next crossing fence. Now continue with a wire fence on the left, with Denbigh below to the left. Bear left to the gate to Gelli [Grove], but then bear right along the hedge to a stile beside a gate. From here a track leads through two fields and then becomes a lane which leads to a road at Berth [Beautiful] Farm.

Turn left and follow the lane down to the B5429. On the way pass a modern house (on the right) and the wood of Wern-fawr on the left, with the farm of Dregoch Ucha [Upper Redtown] opposite. Shortly before the main road there are two more houses, the second of which has a fine covered verandah and balcony facing the view across the vale.

It is possible to turn right along the B5429 back to Waen Aberwheeler, avoiding some field walking and stiles, but the road is busy, particularly with milk tankers. The farm opposite at the road junction is Dregoch Ganol [Middle Redtown], and it has a date of 1712 picked out in brick (partly obscured by an extension) on the side of one building.

3. If not going along the road, cross it to a side road slightly to the left and go down this. Ignore a turning to the right and go round several bends. After a straighter stretch, just after passing a small pond on the right, turn right over a stile which is rather hidden at the top of a small bank (opposite the entrance to Garn Clwyd Bella). Turn right and follow the fence on the right through two fields. Cross a track (which leads to a whitewashed cottage) with stiles each side of it and another soon after. The next stile is obvious across the narrow field and the same direction leads to another stile to the right of Glan Clwyd Ganol [Middle Clwyd Bank] farm.

Go down steps to the right to a concrete area and then cross this to a gate, keeping to the right of all the farm buildings. Go ahead to a stile and continue with a hedge on the right. Leave the field by a stile and pass to the right of a small pond, with a variety of trees (mainly conifers) nearby. Go over another stile and turn right with a fence and stream on the right. Turn left in the field corner. Cross over a stile in the fence and continue, now with the fence on the left. Turn right in the next field corner and go over a stile beside a gate. Turn right up the lane, passing Glan- Clwyd [Clwyd-Bank] farm, to get back into Waen Aberwheeler beside the chapel.

Penycloddiau from Trefechan

A long climb to a fascinating large Iron Age fort with fine views. Some farmland, some lanes with flower-rich hedge-rows.

Distance: *7¼ miles (with an extra ½ mile if starting from the A541).*

Start: *Begin at the hamlet of Trefechan [Little Town], Grid ref: 141 708 (Landranger 116, Pathfinder 755 - 772 also needed for the walk). Parking is available on the road north or south of the hamlet, and also on the A541 nearby.*

By bus: *The 14 bus between Mold and Denbigh (M & H Coaches) runs along the A541. The alighting point is approximately ¾ mile east of Afon-wen and 2 miles northwest of Nannerch, near a telephone box. There are no direction signs, either to Trefechan or, in the other direction, to Ddol. Walk south down the road to the starting point.*

The Route

1. Coming from the A54 just beyond the buildings of Trefechan (including a house with a dovecote in the garden) a footpath sign will be seen in the right hand hedge. Go over the stile, through the gate opposite and down the field to a wooden footbridge in the bottom right hand corner. Cross this and climb the concrete steps beyond to a lane, which is intermittently tarmacked. Turn left up the lane. Pass the drive to a house with a corrugated iron roof on the right.

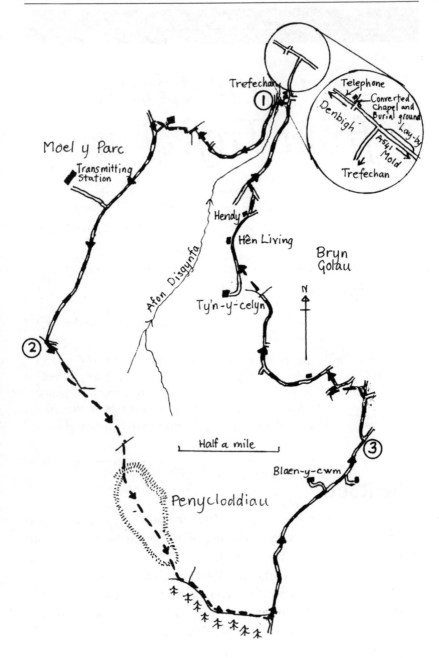

When the lane levels out the impressive bulk of Penycloddiau [Hill of Trenches] can be seen between the trees on the left. Further to the left, across the valley of the Afon Disgynfa [River Descent] is Bryn Golau [Light Hill].

When the main track bends right to a farm, continue on a path with a hedge mainly of holly on the left and a wire fence on the right. Come out into a field and continue with the hedge on the left. The mast of the transmitting station on Moel y Parc [Park Hill] is prominent ahead. Just before a crossing hedge and fence turn left over a stile. Keep the hedge on the right up the next small field and cross the stile which should be at the top by the time this book is published. Keep close to the fence into the corner and turn left along the next stretch, with the hedge on the right including blackthorne and hazel.

Cross the next stile and pass two gates on the right before turning right at the angle of the fence to a stile. Cross this and the one across the farm drive. Unfortunately there is no right of way along the farm drive, which would save some distance and climbing. Bear left across and then down the field, the direction being slightly to the right of a parking area in the wood ahead, to reach a stile in the hedge. Go over this and down to a road. Turn left up the well-surfaced road past a military training area on the right.

The view to the left across the Afon Disgynfa is ever changing. Depending on the time of year you may be able to refresh yourself with raspberries or blackberries from the right hand hedgerow.

The tarmac road turns right into the transmitting station, but the route continues up a reasonable track. *Penycloddiau is now seen more clearly half left across a network of fields which are probably full of sheep.* The track levels off and even descends slightly before it reaches the Offa's Dyke Path, with its acorn waymarks, near the remains of a stand of pines.

2. Cross the facing stile and turn left on the path up Penycloddiau. The route bends about slightly, but it is well waymarked. In a dip is a stile apparently dedicated to the memory of Arthur Roberts MBE. *Beside it is a memorial stone describing him as a guardian of the country, with involvement in the Society for walking the ODP and the Ramblers Holidays campaign to safeguard rural Wales.* At the top of the climb, the three ditches giving the hill its name are crossed, the last rampart being climbed by means of a strange construction of wood and stone, which is presumably to protect from erosion, and the Iron Age hill fort is entered.

You have already seen the greatest earthworks, as it was not felt necessary to defend the other sides to the same extent, because of natural fortifications and steeper slopes. (You may not feel at present that this is true! Never mind—the rest of the walk is mostly downhill!) It is difficult to appreciate the vast size of the fort—over fifty acres—as it cannot all be seen even from the highest point, which is nearby. There have been no major archaeological excavations carried out on the hill.

Unless you are unlucky with the weather, much should be visible on all sides. In the northern quadrant it might be possible to see the spire of the white church at Bodelwyddan [Home of the Wood Spirit], and the sprawl of Prestatyn [Village of the Priests], with the Irish Sea beyond them. The end of the Clwydian Range lies behind Moel y Parc. Further round the Wirral may be seen beyond Flintshire, and possibly the Lancashire coast. The next hill south along the Clwydian Range is Moel Arthur [Arthur's Seat], whose Iron Age fortifications will become more obvious as you head towards them. Obviously higher is Moel Famau [Mothers' Hill], crowned with the remains of its Jubilee Tower. However the finest view is probably to the west. Could the chessboard of fields below in the Vale of Clwyd possibly have given Lewis Carroll the idea for the setting of "Alice through the Looking Glass"? On the far side of the Vale is Denbigh, and it is possible that the view will be crowned by Snowdonia.

Leaving the hill fort at Penycloddiau

The path down through the fort is clear, with heather being replaced by bilberry as the main vegetation after a dried-up pond on the left is passed. The fort is left at a stile, and the path goes to the left of a plantation of larches and then firs. *There is a good sheltered spot for a break here.* Eventually the path enters the wood briefly before coming out into a parking area. Turn left here, leaving the Offa's Dyke Path, and continue down the road for about a mile. The land on the right is part of the Moel Famau Country Park, even though Moel Famau itself is three miles away. Part way down the road, the drive to a farm (Blaen-y-cwm) [Top of the Valley] on the left is passed. At the next road junction turn left, continuing to descend.

3. *In season the hedgerows here are particularly rich with flowers.* Where a track goes up to a farm on the right, go through the gate on the left. The right of way meets the hedge on the right at the midpoint power line pole and follows the hedge down. Cross the stream at the bottom of the field and enter the next field to turn half left to a gate at the far end. Turn right down the lane for about 100 yards and then left up a track. Bend round left with the track, still climbing, and pass a track and a whitewashed cottage bedecked in summer with roses and honeysuckle—both on the right.

Just beyond the top of the hill fork right at a junction of tracks. Pass a track up to the right and go through a gate across the track. *The radio mast on Moel y Parc is again prominent, and the outward route can be traced below it.* A track comes in on the left from Ty'n-y-celyn [Holly House], a large farm. *Across the valley is the old house of Colomendy [Dovecote], which has a date of 1663 on it.*

On the descent Hên [Old] Living is next passed, to the left of the track, which is steadily improving. At the next white house, Hendy [Old House], fork left down the hill and turn left again when a track from Maes yr Esgob [Bishop's Field] comes in on the right. A right turn at the road at the bottom leads back to Trefechan in about half a mile.

Foel Fenlli from Llanbedr-Dyffryn-Clwyd

Quite a stiff climb up onto the Clwydian Range and option-
ally to the top of Foel Fenlli, with its Iron Age fort. Fine
views. A pleasant pastoral return.

Distance: *6 miles.*

Start: *Begin in Llanbedr-Dyffryn-Clwyd (on the A494 about 1½
miles east of Ruthin). Other than at the Griffin Hotel the best parking is alongside the churchyard on the B5429. Grid ref: 144 594
(Landranger 116, Pathfinder 788 - 772 also needed for the walk). (A
better place for parking is Bwlch Penbarra, Grid ref: 162 606 (Point
2), but this means finishing the walk with a climb).*

By bus: *B5 Ruthin to Mold operated by GHA Coaches and 76 Ruthin
to Denbigh operated by Arriva Cymru.*

*Llanbedr-Dyffryn-Clwyd [Church of St Peter in the Vale of Clwyd]
has little of note—a hotel, a shop, the PO and the church. This last was
built only in 1863 by John Jesse of Llanbedr Hall (just west of which
are the ruins of the old church). It contains earlier monuments and, in
the porch, part of what may be a 14th century gravestone.*

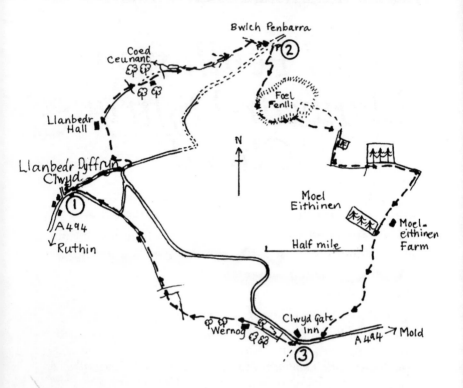

The Route

1. Set off towards Mold along the A494 on the narrow pavement, with Foel Fenlli [Benlli's Hill] in view directly ahead and Moel Eithinen [Gorse Hill] further to the right. *In crossing a stream note the steps on the left down to the water. It was probably an important source of water at one time.* Soon take the little road on the left (Lon Cae Glas [Greenfield Lane]). Take care along here as it carries traffic which has come down from the Bwlch Penbarra pass. Keep left at the road junction, and immediately turn left through a gateway along the private road to Llanbedr Hall, passing Millstream Cottage.

There are soon views to the left across the Vale of Clwyd, over Ruthin [Red Fortress or Red Streak] to a well-forested landscape.

Pass modern houses and turn right through a kissing gate just before a cattle grid. Climb the field, keeping a fence on the right. *The roofs of Llanbedr Hall can be seen behind.* Through a gate enter Coed Ceunant [Wood Gorge], a wood of the Woodland Trust, with a variety of trees. Either pass in front of the white-washed house or take the waymarked permissive path on the left to avoid it. After leaving the wood pass to the right of a pond and the stream that feeds it. Cross a stile and then the stream. The gradient is gentle at first, but steadily increases. Cross a track which contours across the stream and continue up to a stile where the grass changes to gorse and heather. Bear right along a better track to a road and then turn left along the road to the crest at Bwlch Penbarra.

The pass of Bwlch Penbarra [Spur Top Pass], lying between Moel Famau [Mothers' Hill] to the left and Foel Fenlli to the right was the main route between Mold and Ruthin before the creation of the A494, and it may be Roman in origin.

2. Before the cattle grid turn right. The Offa's Dyke Path (ODP) acorn waymarks indicate a path which slopes up to the right, and then zigzags before reaching the fortification ditches and mounds of Foel Fenlli.

The fort contained 35 hut circles and had its own spring. It was ¾ mile across and 24 acres in extent. The fortifications had a height difference from bottom of ditch to top of bank of 35 feet. Legend tells that the citadel of King Benlli was situated here. After the king refused hospitality to Saint Germanus he received divine retribution in the shape of a bolt of lightning. Excavations have found much Roman pottery and coinage. The fort is regarded as being late Iron Age or Romano-British. Across the Vale of Clwyd the Berwyn [Foaming or Passion] Mountains may be seen to the left of Ruthin and the peaks of Snowdonia to the right. As you climb the remains of the tower on Moel Famau can be seen to the north.

Looking down to Ruthin from Bwlch Penbarra

Climb up through the lower ditches and then follow them round the hillside to a sharp little climb, at the top of which the ODP turns right.

I was entertained to a wonderful aerobatic display here by a pair of ravens. It was an enhanced combination of the Red Arrows (without the noise), Torville and Dean, and Fonteyn and Nureyev!

Continue the climb ahead if you wish to reach the top with its views over the Dee and the Mersey to Liverpool. You can then descend another rough path to rejoin the ODP at a point where it turns right.

The combined path goes down over two stiles and climbs slightly beside a conifer wood (on the left). Cross another stile and descend to a gate. Turn left before this and continue to descend with a fence on the right. Climb a stile and keep to the right of another block of conifers. *To the left here the scenic area of the Loggerheads Country Park can be seen.* At the corner of the field turn right, as indicated by the ODP waymarks and soon keep to the right of a row of hawthorns. Continue with Moel Eithinen to the right, and the farm of the same name to the left to pass through a strip of woodland. Shortly bear right along a farm track and continue down through gates and over cattle grids (or stiles if you happen to be a masochist) until the A494 is reached. Turn right along this until directly below the Clwyd Gate Inn.

3. Cross the road here with great care and set off down the little road opposite, which is the ODP. Leave this only 20 yards from the road, going over a stile on the right. Walk down the field with a fence on the right and the Vale of Clwyd ahead. Enter a small wood by means of another stile. The path has a fence on the left and, later, a track joins from the right. Continue ahead, passing to the right of Gwernyd [Alder Groves], and then bear gently left to pass through another stretch of woodland. Leave the woodland by a stile and head half right to a stile in the next crossing hedge.

It is not easy to find the correct line through the next field. The safest method is to turn right along the hedge into the corner and then turn left. Look out for a metal gate to the right. Go through this and a belt of scrub to a wooden gate. Beyond this keep to the right of a hedge which is at right angles to the edge of the last field. Keep to this hedge until a gate is reached, beyond a recently-restored house on the left. Through the gate join the drive and follow this to the A494. Turn left along the road. There is soon a footpath on the right-hand side. Return to Llanbedr-Dyffryn-Clwyd, eventually passing "Gate House" (opposite the church), which appears to have been a toll house originally.

Graig-fechan

Initially pleasant farmland, then a moderate climb up onto the Clwydian Range, passing Moel y Plâs and Moel y Gelli before returning to the Vale of Clwyd.

Distance: *6¼ miles.*

Start: *Begin in Graig-fechan [Little Rock] on the B5429, just south of the Three Pigeons Inn. Apart from the inn's large car park, the safest place for parking on this busy road (a main route for milk tankers) is probably further south, near the phone box in the centre of the village. Grid ref: (for the start of the walk) 148 544 (Landranger 116, Pathfinder 788).*

By bus: *Graig-fechan is served by the 76 service from Denbigh and Ruthin (Arriva Cymru). Alight at the Three Pigeons.*

The Route

1. In the depression just south of The Three Pigeons Inn (which has a date of 1777 on it) take a track to the west (ie with the inn on the right). Bypass Tan y Graig [Under the Rock] by using a kissing gate on the left and then two more kissing gates at the other end. Turn left along a track. When this turns left into a sewage treatment works go ahead over a stile into a field. Keep the tree-lined stream on the left and climb the stile into an enclosed track which turns right to Glan-yr-Avon [River Bank]. Immediately after a bridge and level with a low barn on the left, turn right over a hidden stile and keep to the fence on the right.

Ahead some of the Clwydian Range of hills come into sight, Moel Famau [Mothers' Hill] being prominent with the remains of its Jubilee Tower. Below on the right the Dwr Iâl [Upland Water] gurgles along.

Proceed through a second field towards Garthgynan, with its tall chimneys. *Garthgynan is an early example of building in brick, with farm buildings dated 1658 and 1702.* Go out through the gate at the end of this second field, and turn back right on a track. At the ruins of Melin [Mill] Garth-Gynan turn left over the old mill leat and Dwr Iâl itself. Go up through a gate to reach the B5429.

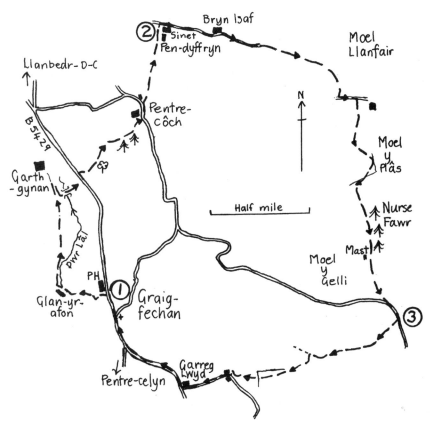

Turn left along the road as far as the end of a stone wall on the right. Turn in through a gate and skirt a group of trees to reach a fence on the right. Beyond the fence is a wood (Coed Henblas [Old Hall Wood]), with interesting rock outcrops. Turn left, with the wood on the right. Beside a rocky outcrop on the left (with a cave on its far side) take a stile on the right. Head towards the far corner of the field. Soon the path has a fence on the left. Go left down a green lane and over a stile to the right of the entrance to Pentre-côch [Red Village] farmyard. Keep the fence on the left to another stile into a road.

Turn left along the road through the pretty hamlet. Take a footpath to the right of the white gates of Plas-tirion [Gracious

The author looking across to Moel y Waun

Hall] at the far end, as the road bends left. Go into the field and turn left along the fence at the back of Plas-tirion (which shows a date of 1909). Keep to the fence to the next crossing fence, where a gate leads to the next field. Keep the hedge on the right through the next field.

The parkland to the left (including a lake which is not shown on maps) probably belongs to Pentre Coch Manor, which can just be seen among trees.

Climb the stile into the next field, where you should keep to the hedge for some time and then aim for a stile in the white railings around the gardens of Pen-dyffryn [Valley Peak]. Go over the stile and then go left along the gravel drive, but shortly turn left and then right (as indicated by a painted FP and arrow low down on a stone wall. (Do not go out through the gates on the left.) The path leads through part of the garden to a stile. Go up past a farm building bearing a tractor windvane and a projecting dovecot. A gate leads onto a road.

2. Turn right up the road past Sinet farm.

The hedges are high and the trees arch overhead, so there are few views on the early part of the climb. In the winter this road must get treacherous—as evidenced by the frequent piles of grit.

Pass Bryn Isaf [Lower Hill] Farm, with its Swiss-style barn conversion, and continue up on a track, which gets rougher.

Soon there is a view ahead of some of the Clwydian Range, with Moel Llanfair [St Mary's Hill] to the left and Moel y Plâs [Hall Hill] to the right. Take heart!—the route goes to the summit of neither. Eventually there is also a fine view behind over the Vale of Clwyd with Ruthin to the right and the vast Clocaenog Forest—frequently used in the RAC Rally—further away to the left.

The track emerges and proceeds between wire fences, with improved views in all directions, and the gradient lessens until the last section as it bends right to meet a less prominent track.

A left turn up this leads to the col between Moel Llanfair [St Mary's Church Hill] and Moel y Plâs.

The Offa's Dyke Path (ODP) is joined here, but there is more climbing to come. Go over a stile on the right to climb the brackeny slopes of Moel y Plâs.

If refreshment or rest is needed there is a very convenient bank (part of a tumulus) just over the stile with what appear to be extensive stable buildings below. Don't miss the opportunity of a view westwards, with Loggerheads prominent in the valley below and limestone quarries in several hills behind.

Soon heather tends to take over from the bracken. *Below the summit of Moel y Plâs the first of three steep valleys goes down to the Vale of Clwyd. The V shape indicates a lack of glacial activity.*

As you reach a stile Moel y Gelli [Grove Hill] is ahead. After crossing the stile there is access to the top of Moel y Plâs to the left, but the ODP initially follows the fence to the right and then turns left down the slope. The fishing lake of Llyn Gweryd [Earth Pool] (passed on Walk 8) comes into sight on the left and, after a ladder stile is climbed, the top of another valley is passed. *Across the Vale of Clwyd on a clear day there will be glimpses of distant mountains.*

The path goes between a communications mast and Nurse Fawr [Great Nursery], the wood on the left. Behind the mast the hill is Moel y Gelli. The path switchbacks down a ridged field and meets a track from the left (part of Walk 8). Continue to a road which has come up the near shoulder of yet another valley going down to the Vale of Clwyd.

3. Our route goes along the road for few yards then over a stile or through a gate on the right and continues along a track with a fence on the left. The track passes a small quarry and goes through a gate in a small depression. The track now becomes enclosed. Pass two gates on the right within about 100 yards and then two gates on the left similarly close. Turn left over a stile and follow the fence on the left for a short distance (to the top of the slope of what appears to be another tumulus) before bearing right to a gate in a transverse fence and then keeping to the left of sheep pens on the skyline. Past the sheep pens bear right along a fence until a stile can be seen in the next transverse fence.

From here there are splendid views—ahead across the Vale of Clwyd and behind to Moel y Waun [Moor Hill].

From the stile take a faint path ahead. This crosses a number of more prominent paths and for the most part goes along the boundary between bracken and gorse, but it does cut through a tongue of gorse. Towards the bottom of the hill the path comes out above a track which has recently been cut into the shaly hillside. Go to the right along the track to a stile in the fence on the left. Go over this and turn back left down a rough lane.

Turn sharply back right along a surfaced lane, and soon turn left at a corner. Follow the lane down from the corner to a T-junction. *Garreg Lwyd [Grey Rock] here now houses "Phil's Auto Repairs and Servicing".* Turn right here down the road, passing a striking modern extension to a bungalow before the road joins the B5429 near more modern houses. Keep on through Graigfechan to return to the start.

Llandegla and the River Alun

Pleasant undulating countryside, with lots of limestone out-crops.

Distance: *8 miles from Llandegla. (The walk can also be done from Llanarmon-yn-Ial in which case the distance is 8½ miles.)*

Start: *Begin in Llandegla. There is a car park near the church, on the right approaching from the A5104. Grid ref: 196 524 (Landranger 116, Pathfinder 788—Landranger 117 or Pathfinder 789 also needed for walk). Parking in Llanarmon-yn-Ial is less satisfactory. Start from the west gateway into the churchyard. Grid ref: 190 562.*

By bus: *Llandegla is served by the D8 (Ruthin/Corwen to Wrexham) and 91 (Bettws Gwerfil Goch to Wrexham) services, both run by G H A Coaches. Llanarmon-yn-Ial has better bus services—B5 between Ruthin and Mold (G H A Coaches) and E12 to Wrexham (George Edwards & Son).*

Llandegla [Church of St Tecla] is a small village, with few facilities except for the Post Office and shop. The ancient well of St Tecla was famous for curing diseases by a complicated process involving the disease being transferred to a cock or hen. Bronze Age burial urns have been found nearby. The present church was built only in 1866, probably by the same architect as the "Marble Church" at Bodelwyddan, and is dedicated to St Tecla, who was converted to Christianity by St Paul and subsequently martyred by the Romans. Inside the church are an old font, a brass chandelier topped by the figure of the Virgin Mary,

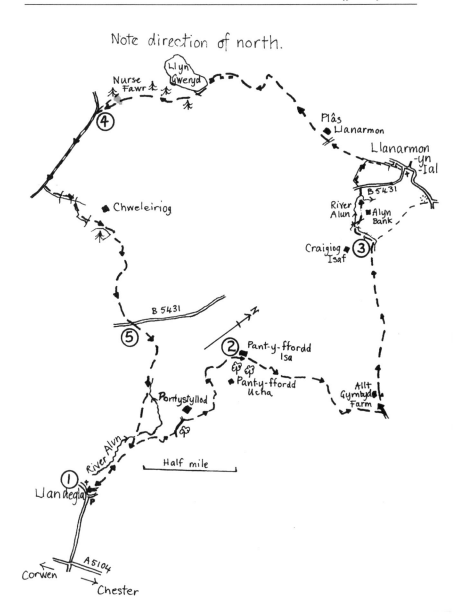

Note direction of north.

Llyn Gweryd

Nurse Fawr

④

Plâs Llanarmon

Llanarmon -yn -Ial

B 5431

River Alun

Alyn Bank

Chweleiriog

Craigiog Isaf

③

B 5431

N

⑤

② Pant-y-ffordd Isa

Pant-y-ffordd Ucha

Allt Gymbyd Farm

Pontystyllod

River Alvn

Half mile

① Llandegla

A 5104

Corwen

Chester

which is reputed to have come from Valle Crucis Abbey at its dissolution, and a very unusual east window of 1800 full of cherubs. This is of "burnt glass" and is supposed to have come from St Asaph Cathedral.

In the 19th Century the village was famed as the meeting place of many drovers' roads. Welsh Black cattle were brought from all over North Wales through this area to be sold in the English markets. At that time every other house in the village was an ale house. Now there isn't one!

The Route

1. Start off, heading north along the Offa's Dyke Path (as indicated by the acorn waymarks) along the track to the right of the church and the left of the wistaria-bearing Old Rectory. Pass a small sewage works on the left and then go over a stile into a field. Keep to the right of the coppiced trees, which prove to be on the banks of the River Alun. *[Alun is a common name for a river, being associated with the old Celtic god and river Alaunos. It may also relate to its meandering nature.]* Continue with the river on the left until a footbridge is seen on the left. Instead of going over this take a stile to the right.

Keep to the right of the line of trees ahead to reach the meandering Alun again, and when the river bends left keep ahead over an extremely small stone bridge over a stream and a stile in the fence on the right. Follow the fence on the left to another stile beside a metal gate. From this go ahead to another metal gate, which leads out onto the lane to Pontystyllod [Plank Bridge] farm. Bear left along the lane, passing a mixed plantation on the right. At the farm gate take a stile on the right and go up on the edge of the wood behind a barn. Leave the wood by a stile and turn right to another stile beside a wooden gate, which leads into a field with low limestone outcrops. Keep to the right of a tree-topped bank ahead until there is a gap in the bank and then turn left across a narrow stretch of grass to a stile. Descend from this with a fence on the left, curving round to the right.

Burnt glass window and chandelier in Llandegla church

When a group of buildings with a tennis court and swimming pool is in sight turn left through a gate and again descend with a fence on the left. Go through another gate and keep ahead to a stile on the right of a large tree. Over the stile turn right to a track leading up to Pant-y-Ffordd Ucha [Upper Road Valley]. Turn left along the track, which soon bends right.

It may be possible, through the trees on the left to see Moel y Gelli [Grove Hill], with a transmitting mast, and Moel y Plâs [Hall Hill].

The track leads down to another farm (presumably Lower Road Valley).

2. When the track swings left, go right with a bridleway sign through a bridle gate, and join the track from the farm after going through another gate. The track goes up through another gate into a rough field. Follow the bridleway signs up this, keeping to the right of the field. At the top of the field a wooden gate leads into an enclosed track, which winds about, with a broken stone wall and fence always on the left, bearing right when there are caravans over to the left. Further on the track turns left and goes through a gate. After more bends, with limestone and scrubby trees on the right, the track levels off and then descends, with the buildings of Allt Gymbyd farm to the left. *There is a fine view to the left down over the farm to Moel Famau [Mothers' Hill] in the Clwydian Range. Craig Quarry is nearer.* Bear left through a gateway onto a road.

Go left through the gateway to Allt Gymbyd, between the lion-topped gateposts. Keep to the left of the first low building and to the right of the others. *The farmhouse is dated 1789.* Keep down the right of the next field, which also holds the first hole of a golf course. Keep the same sort of fence on the right for the next few fields. Drop down into the next field, and keep to the right of the second tee. Keep on through intermittent light woodland and in the next field keep to the right of the fourth hole. Go through another strip of woodland, with a stile at either side, and then ignore a stile on the right, which leads into an extensive caravan site.

Cross the remains of a wall which appears to have been made of bits of limestone pavement. Curve round to the right to the next stile, which is a ladder with five steps up and eight down. Keep further from the fence in the next field to an even bigger ladder—eight steps on each side. At the end of the next field the route splits. (To reach Llanarmon-yn-Ial [Church of St Germanus in the Upland] go ahead for nearly half a mile to reach a road. To reach the village turn left past Tomen y Phedre [Mound of the Dairy Hamlet).

This is the remains of the motte of an old castle, which may have been a 11th century local administrative centre. Llanarmon-yn-Ial has a pub (The Raven Inn) and a Post Office. The church has twin naves with fine window tracery, recumbent effigies from the 13th century and a mediaeval brass chandelier.)

3. To bypass Llanarmon on a delightful path turn left, with, on the right, first a hedge, then a hedge and wall, and finally a wall topped with intimidating barbed wire. The path descends between limestone outcrops. *To the left is Creigiog-isaf [Lower Rocky], with a stepped gable.*

Bear right over a stile. The River Alun is to the left, with a stone slab footbridge over it. Do not cross the bridge, but go ahead over a metal stile. Proceed between the babbling river and a house, Alyn Bank. Get onto the lane from Alyn Bank at a stile in the hedge on the right and turn left along it, crossing the Alun, to reach a road. Go across the road to a stile. Go along the left hand edge of a field to the corner, then turn right and continue to the next corner, where turn left. Ignore the next paragraph.

(If starting from Llanarmon-yn-Ial cross the road from the west gate into the churchyard. Go over a stone stile by a sign to Nurse Fawr [Great Nursery]. Follow the path through a wooden gate to come out into a new bungalow development. Take a path to the right of the bungalow at the opposite end. This leads to an awkward stile into a field. Follow the hedge on the left for a few yards, and then take a stile to transfer to the other side of the hedge. Continue in the same direction to the next hedge to join the route from Llandegla.)

Go over two stiles, keeping the hedge on the right. Then head for a marker post to the right of a mound that looks like a tumulus and continue to a stile which leads into a lane. Take the track opposite past Plâs-Llanarmon [Llanarmon Hall]. *Llanarmon-yn-Ial can now be seen behind.* The track bends left and right, with a fine view developing across the valley to the heathery slopes of Moel Garagog [Stony Hill] and the wooded Fron

Hafod [Hillside Summer Dwelling]. Pass above the Llyn Gweryd [Earth Pool] fishery office and bear left at the gates of the Gweryd Lodge Estate to pass the end of the pool. Continue along the path when the track goes left and go through a gate onto a good track through a recently planted area of conifers. The track bends right, now with open views to the left and the wood of Nurse Fawr on the right. A gate leads onto the Offa's Dyke Path (ODP), which goes left to a minor road. *(Point 3 on walk 7).*

4. Turn left along the road, after admiring the view west to the Vale of Clwyd, with ranges of hills behind, including the knobbly Foel Goch [Red Hill] to the left. Soon after the crest of the hill take a stile on the left with an acorn waymark. Keep to the hedge on the right and pass over three stiles in quick succession (which is typical of much of the ODP). A stile in the right hand hedge leads to a descending path which is a recent change to the ODP, and which avoids Chweleiriog [Land abounding in maggots or vipers]. Keep to the wandering hedgeline on the right to a stile and across the next field to the left hand end of a copse. Bear right to the farm track. Go right along this, and continue along it as it meanders through sheep pastures to the B5431.

5. Cross the road to a stile opposite and go down a green lane. The path turns right into a field and keeps to the left hand edge. It then goes right, with the remains of a hedge on the left until it meets a fence. Go left here and then soon right over a stile. Bear left towards the River Alun (which, except after rain, is no more than a clear brook with a shingle bed). When the river goes left, cross a footbridge over a ditch. Continue ahead, with a ladder stile for a change, and then a plantation on the left. Cross the "river" itself and then turn right with it, rejoining the outward route. From time to time Llandegla is glimpsed ahead, and it is eventually entered past the church.

Valle Crucis Abbey and the Eglwyseg Valley

A lovely walk, full of interest, with abbey and castle ruins, towering limestone cliffs and valleys large and small.

Distance: *7½ miles (5 miles by taking a short cut).*

Start: *Except for the limited parking at the abbey itself the nearest parking to Valle Crucis Abbey is a small parking area on the A542 about 200 yards north of the junction with the B5103. It is on the left of the road going north, and has a footpath sign to Coed Hyrddyn [Velvet Hill]. Grid ref: 204 439 (Landranger 117, Pathfinder 806).*

By bus: *On Tuesdays and Fridays only the 98 service runs from Llangollen (Bryn Melyn Motor Services). Alight at Valle Crucis Abbey and walk down to the abbey to join the route. (It is slightly shorter to walk into Llangollen than to complete the circuit.)*

The Route

1. From the car park walk north along the A542 for about 100 yards and then take a footpath on the right to Valle Crucis Abbey.

This Cistercian abbey was founded in 1201 but was badly damaged by fire and not rebuilt until about 50 years later. At the dissolution of the monasteries by Henry VIII part became a farmhouse. The abbey is now in the care of Cadw and the ruins are worth a tour if time permits. It is also photogenic if the caravan sites can be avoided. (I suppose, to be *charitable, the caravan sites **could** be regarded as a continuation of the monastic custom of succour for travellers!) The name (Abbey of the Vale of the Cross) relates to a cross set up in memory of Eliseg, Prince of Powys in the 9th century. Its remains (The Pillar of Eliseg) are on the east of the A542 about ¼ mile north of the abbey.*

Before the Ice Age a great loop of the River Dee came round the north side of Coed Hyrddyn, flowing back through Valle Crucis into its present valley, which the river has since lowered. The remains of a glacier prevented the river from taking its earlier route and forced it to cut through the neck of Coed Hyrddyn.

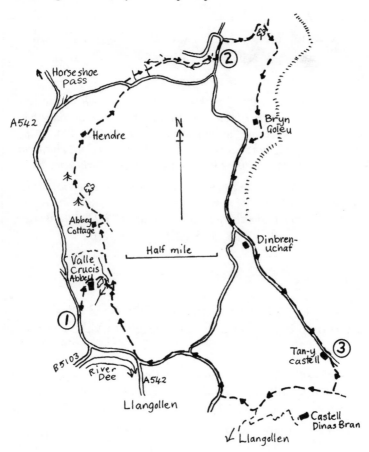

Go to the left of the abbey into a caravan site. Keep along the track to the right and, as the Eglwyseg [Church's] River is approached, a path will be seen leading to a bridge. *The abbey fish pond can be seen on the right before the bridge.* Cross the bridge and go up the new path angling to the right up the steep slope, mostly with wood-edged steps. At the top turn left along a level track. Keep on the left of the field, above the river. Note an unusual iron ladder stile on the left, but don't go over it. At Abbey Cottage go over a wooden ladder stile and turn right. Another ladder stile leads to a level track where you turn left again.

The track begins to climb between trees, with tightly packed conifers on the left and more scattered deciduous trees on the right. Further up the gentle slope, with only a fence on the left, there are good views of the valley of a tributary of the Eglwyseg, with the A542 going up to Horseshoe Pass. Pass Hendre [Winter dwelling] and ignore two more paths to the left before dropping down to a road.

By now the limestone cliffs to the right and ahead will have been seen, looking, in the right lighting conditions, like a backdrop for a western movie.

Turn left at the road, passing between the buildings of Tan-y-fron [Under the hillside] farm. Take the next gate on the right, go along the slope to the higher of two gaps in a hawthorn hedge and then aim towards a prominent ash tree by a gateway. Pass through this into the next field and keep ahead to the bank of the Eglwyseg River, which is now much narrower, without the benefit of the water from the Horseshoe Pass valley. Go over a footbridge and turn right through what may be a boggy section. Go over a stile and turn left to another one, which has been a gate. Turn right on a better track. Pass what has probably been a mill, now restored, and other buildings to join the track from these. Cross over the river and go through a gate.

2. Turn left along the road, unless you wish to avoid some climbing and a stretch across the steep hillside, in which case turn right. At Plas yn Eglwyseg [Church's Hall], with its uncompromising, solid buildings, turn right over a stile with a footpath waymark. The steepest climb of the walk goes up the left side of the field to a gate about 100 yards before the angle of the wood. Go through the gate and turn right to follow the fence and then the wood edge until a marker post is reached. (Seen from the other direction the arrow on this seems to demand an aerial takeoff!)

If there is a need for a break the view behind gives ample excuse. Across the valley is Maesyrychen [Field of oxen] Mountain, whose highest point is Moel y Gamelin [Camel Hill].

Follow the waymarks up through a short stretch of woodland with coppiced trees and tangled trunks, at the top of which cross a stile and turn right. Keep to the fence on the right, going through a gate of hurdles if necessary and the Offa's Dyke Path (ODP) will eventually be joined.

The cliffs above are most impressive, and the thought of climbing them (as many do) quite hair-raising, especially in view of the number of rocks (some of them barely distinguishable from the sheep) which have fallen off, mostly in the Ice Age. Still, there are a surprising number of trees growing from cracks in the crags, so there must be handholds! The cliffs (three bands of hard white limestone separated by narrow bands of shale) were formed by the Aqueduct Fault (one of a number in the area).

The path now slants upward among scree, but shouldn't be dangerous except in bad weather. It is well cut even if exposed. The path passes a rather isolated form of civilisation at Bryn Goleu [Light Hill]. Above the house is a tree encased in a stone wall, which may once have been a lime kiln—there would certainly have been plenty of stone to feed it, and there was also coal nearby. Another river of rock is crossed and the path goes

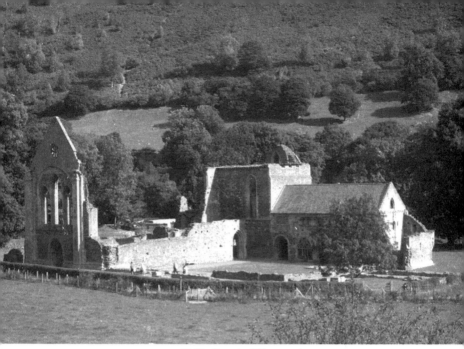

Valle Crucis Abbey

down to a road. Turn left. The ODP follows this road for nearly three miles, but we will be turning off after 1¼.

As you come round a corner the ruins of Castell Dinas Bran [The Hill Fort of Bran] appear in silhouette, looking for all the world like a modern folly, rather than the remains of a castle built about 700 years ago. The likely builder, Madoc ap Gruffydd Maelor, was also the founder of Valle Crucis Abbey. The hill on which it stands is composed of Silurian mudstones.

Ignore the road on the right signposted to Llangollen unless you want the shorter route back to Valle Crucis Abbey. The longer route continues along the road to the left, over a cattle grid and passes above the farm of Dinbren-uchaf [Upper hill-fortress].

3. The next farm on the right (in about ¾ mile) is Tan-y-castell, and it is here we leave the road and the ODP. (For the last mile or so the route has coincided with that for Walk 10, which explores some of the less frightening limestone slopes above.) Just past the farm turn right down a path with a white (permissive) arrow. Pass to the right of a building clad in corrugated metal and then turn right just before what may possibly be another old lime kiln. Go over a stile to the right then down the middle of the field to cross a stream and go up to another footpath. Turn right on this over a stile.

The path skirts the bottom of the castle mound. When the trees on the right cease the prominent building across the valley to the right is Dinbren Hall. A path splitting off to the left is a quick way back into Llangollen [Church of St Collen], which could be useful for anyone who has gone from there by bus. It is also the way for anyone with spare energy to reach the path up to the castle ruins. The return route to Valle Crucis Abbey keeps to the right through bracken beside the fence to a stile which leads into a field. The right of way through the field keeps to the right edge to a gate and stile in the far corner. Over the stile turn right along a road.

At the top of a rise the road on the right is the end of the short cut signposted to Llangollen and the entrance to Dinbren Hall is on the left. ["Dinbren" may have the same derivation as "Dinas Bran"]. The hall was once occupied by the Rev Edward Roberts and his wife, who were friends of the famous "Ladies of Llangollen". The ruined buildings nearby are the remains of a quarry.

Keep on the road to Ruthin, which descends to the A542. Turn right here. It is possible to follow the main road to the car park, but it is more pleasant and safer to take a footpath on the right just beyond the entrance to Llwyn Palis [Wainscot Grove]. Go over the stile beside the gate and along the obvious stony track. There are two more gates with stiles and then the track bends left and right. There are two paths on the left which lead down to the bridge to the abbey, the second being down the newly engineered steps. Return as you came out, through the caravan site and past the abbey entrance. To get back to cars parked by the A542 take the kissing gate opposite the abbey and return to the far left corner of the field.

Panorama Walk from Trevor

One loop pastoral and wooded, the other among limestone outcrops, with lovely views of the Vale of Llangollen.

Distance: *7¼ miles, in loops of 3¼ and 4 miles.*

Start: *Begin in Trevor [Great Hamlet] on the A539 between Llangollen and Ruabon. The best place to park is on the road which leaves the A539 at the Australia Arms public house. This climbs and turns right, before straightening and widening to provide safe parking. Grid ref: about 264 424 (Landranger 117, Pathfinder 806). For the second loop there are numerous parking spots on the Panorama Walk road between 223 439 and 246 428.*

By bus: *Buses which run along the A539 through Trevor are the X5 and 5 between Wrexham and Llangollen (Bryn Melyn on weekdays and Arriva Cymru on Sundays) and the 94 between Wrexham and Barmouth via Llangollen, Corwen and Dolgellau (Arriva Cymru). In either case alight at Trevor Post Office. Go up the road opposite the Post Office, beside the Australia Arms, and bear right to the starting point.*

The Route

1. Walk up the road to Garth [Enclosure, headland or ridge], taking care as there are no pavements, and the road is quite busy. Pass a War Memorial on the right (unusually the deaths in the Second World War were nearly as high as in the first) and

The Rockmans Arms (presumably referring to a major local industry) on the left. *Views across the Vale of Llangollen to the wooded slopes opposite are starting to develop on the left as you climb.* Just after a notable terraced garden on the right, and below a converted chapel, turn left, ignoring the "Panorama" sign to the right.

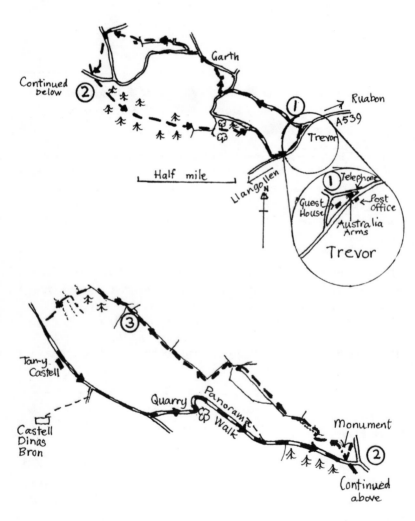

When the end of speed limit sign is seen ahead turn right across a grass patch in front of a cottage. Climb the fence ahead and turn right beside a thick cypress hedge. At the field corner bear left with an old hedge on the right. Work your way to the left round the incongruous grey wall of a new bungalow to a fence which is easily climbed and go up the slope to another fence. Over this you are on a tarmacked path which leads up to the road opposite a play area. This is Garth. Turn left up the road, bearing right past another converted chapel.

Fork left at the next junction along Ffordd Pen-y-Gaer [Hillfort Road] Road, which is narrow but well-surfaced. Again just before the end-of-restriction signs turn right into Ffordd Maes Mawr [Great Field Road] Road. Follow this up to a sharp right bend, where you go ahead through a gate and across the field to the fence in line with a power line pole.

Behind there is now a fine view of the River Dee, spanned by the Pont Cysyllte [Junction Bridge] canal aqueduct and the railway bridge behind.

Continue with a fence on the left through two fields to a fence in the corner. Over this bear to the right of a bungalow, through a patch which in summer may be overgrown by bracken. Cross the track from the garage of the bungalow and find a much better path through the next patch of bracken. This leads to a fence into a field. Cross this, keeping to the left of a holiday chalet, and then bear right to a proper stile (at last!).

Turn left along the road for about 100 yards and then go left at a T-junction. Soon, take the signed path to the right over a new stile complete with dog gate. Within 100 yards take the path on the left through bracken, bilberry and heather and then through a small clump of silver birch. *(Some of them are old and "tarnished", with their bark rough and lichened.)* At a three-way fingerpost on the crest of the hill continue with the yellow ar-

Castell Dinas Bran from the lane near Tan y Castell

row, going down with a splendid view of the Vale of Llangollen [Church of St Collen] over the conifers. Before the conifers is a road.

2. From here it is possible to return to Trevor, following the instructions from "2 again." To continue follow the permissive path up to the monument.

This is to an I D Hooson (1880 - 1948), and refers to him as a bard, frequenter of eisteddfods and friend of Welsh children. The spot must have been chosen for the glorious view of the Vale of Llangollen, with the ruins of Castell Dinas Bran [The Hill Fort of Bran] showing for the first time.

Follow the path upwards to a large isolated rock and then, more steeply, to the limestone escarpment. Take a right fork to reach a good path behind the summit rocks. Turn left along this, climbing with a decrepit stone wall on the right. Cross this when it reaches the edge and proceed to a prominent cairn.

From here there are also views to the north, with a pastoral land-scape beyond the fringe of moor.

Beyond the cairn the path continues to rise. When the wall forks, follow the right hand branch to a fence. Slant left with this and bear right to the next corner. Here the only permitted way is down—quite steeply—with a view over old quarries to Castell Dinas Bran and Llangollen. At the bottom there is another fingerpost. Take the permissive path to the right. This rises again across a moor with, in the summer, purple bell heather and golden gorse combining in imperial splendour. Cross a stile but keep the same line, with traces of a wall on the right, ignoring a number of crossing paths, to reach a maze of fences on what had been the skyline.

3. Keep to the left of a sheep pen and climb the ladder stile to regain the previous line. Keep to the fence on the left, behind which are the coniferous remains of Eglwyseg [Church's] Plantation. Keep along the fence to a stile. Cross over this and go down alongside the plantation. Cross a track to the next fingerpost. (If the grass is wet it is safer to turn left down the track, which reaches the Panorama Walk road at the hairpin.) The faint track ahead, which is not signed, goes down through bracken, and it is sometimes easier to walk on bits of an old wall. Below the bracken the path leads down through successive bands of limestone crags, separated by bands of shale. (This is seen most impressively from below.) It is advisable to cross the stream to the right **above** the slippery rocks at the second band of crags. Care is needed throughout this descent, particularly in wet weather. Pick the best route, keeping fairly close to the stream bed until you arrive at a narrow road. Turn left along it, joining the Offa's Dyke Path (ODP).

This is the Panorama Walk, and the changing views into and across the Vale of Llangollen are a feature of the next 1½ miles, including the River Dee and, on its further side, the A5 trunk road. At first the view to the right is dominated by the hill crowned by the ruins of Castell Dinas Bran. Earthworks put the history of this back to the Bronze Age, but the present ruined buildings date from the reign of Henry III. For the next 100 years the castle featured in history, being captured by Edward I, only to be restored to the Welsh and again captured following the great Welsh rising of 1282.

If the legs and lungs allow it is possible to make a detour to the ruins and return to the Panorama Walk on an obvious path which starts over a cattle grid after the hill has been passed.

Earlier what looked from a distance to be a Welsh name by the roadside, turned out to read "LANDSLIDE", indicating that the road is liable to be covered in debris tumbling down the steep slopes on the left.

Ignore a fork downhill to the right. The ODP road climbs fairly steadily past Trevor Rocks and the old quarry area and goes round a small hairpin in crossing a stream coming down from Eglwyseg Plantation.

The hillside to the right is pleasantly wooded, but the steel mesh boxes filled with stones indicate that the instability of the hillside has caused problems.

Where the next path comes down on the left maps tend to show the Offa's Dyke Path forking right, but it does in fact follow the road up, mostly above a large conifer plantation. Path signs to the left indicate that we have returned to:-

2.(again) Just beyond, a waymark indicates where the ODP goes down into the wood. As the path descends in the gloomy depths of the wood the only cheerful aspects are the coos and twitterings of birds. For a while the path goes along an open ride, thick with brambles (and, in season, blackberries), but it slides back into another band of conifers to continue the descent. The path returns to daylight, with a deciduous wood on the right and the buildings of Garth visible up the hillside to the left, and then enters the wood, going down a rough path past a variety of trees. When the path meets a track turn left and go through a pair of white gateposts.

Presumably these led to the demolished Trevor Hall, which was the ancestral home of the influential Trevor family until they moved to Brynkinalt near Chirk. The hall had been built in the 17th century. Trefor Church, built about 1717 as a private chapel, was consecrated in 1772. It is back along the track and then to the left. A simple rectangular structure, except for what appears to be a crypt tacked on the SW corner, it is normally locked, but a key is usually available in Garth. In spite of being some distance from Trevor itself there are weekly services.

Follow a small road down right to the A539 and turn left again. The ODP can be seen going off to the right. Bus stops are ahead along the A539, but to return to cars parked up the road to Garth take the first lane on the left and then turn left again.

Froncysyllte

A stretch of the Llangollen Canal followed by a climb up to Fron Isaf, with sections of Offa's Dyke and views of the Vale of Llangollen and Chirk.

Distance: *3½ miles.*

Start: *Begin at the junction of A5 and B5434. Grid ref: 272 413 (Landranger 117, Pathfinder 806). (The walk also goes briefly onto Landranger 126, Pathfinder 827.) There are lay-bys with parking for up to four hours on the A5 at the east end of the town and further parking down the B5434 near the canal.*

By bus: *The weekday 64 bus between Llangollen and Glyn Ceiriog and the 96 (Weds and Sats) from Llangollen to Oswestry (both Bryn Melyn) go through Froncysyllte. The main stop is near the start of the walk.*

Froncysyllte [Junction Hillside] clings to the side of the valley above the Vale of Llangollen. It owes its existence to the closeness of the A5 and the canal. Its church (St David's) dates only from 1870, with a new chancel being added in 1914. Half a mile along the B5434 towards Trevor is the old Cysylltau [Junctions] bridge across the River Dee. From here can be seen the best view of Telford's magnificent aqueduct carrying the Llangollen branch of the Shropshire Union Canal 121 feet above the river. The valley of the River Dee was originally formed by faults causing a section of the land to sink.

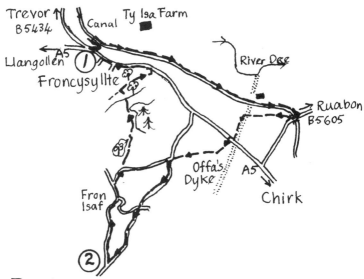

The Route

1. Take a road branching from the A5 at the same point as the B5434, but to the right of it. This zigzags down to the canal. Cross the canal by one of the bridges and turn right along the towpath on the Offa's Dyke Path (ODP).

Looking to the right across the valley is a railway viaduct and to the left is the canal aqueduct—which is not easily recognisable because of not being able to see between the piers. The area beyond is largely industrial.

The towpath starts off as a gravelled track which soon turns left into Ty Isa [Lower House] Farm, but continues in normal fashion. *The structure across the canal beyond the moorings is probably a set of limekilns.* Soon the canal is between fields, but the traffic on the A5 can be seen and heard.

For a good distance the banks of the canal are reinforced with concrete. Offa's Dyke crosses just beyond this, being more easily seen as a tree-topped bank across the canal. This is the most northerly point where the ODP and the Dyke meet.

Newbridge railway viaduct from Cloud Hill

The towpath again becomes a gravel track, coming from buildings abutting the line of the Dyke. Follow the track up to the B5605 road. Turn right over the bridge and again right over a stile into a field. Diverge gradually from the canal, through one hedgerow to meet the Dyke at a stile about 30 yards up from the canal. Cross the Dyke and turn left over another stile and then keep the Dyke on the left up to the next stile on Cloud Hill. *Looking to the right on the way up the field Trevor Rocks should be in view across the Vale of Llangollen [Church of St Collen].* Go over the stile, drop down to the A5 and turn right on the footway for a short distance.

Across the road can be seen an outlying hill of the Berwyn Range, part of which the walk will climb. Geologically the hill is composed of Silurian flags and slate.

Cross to a waymarked stile of an unusual stone and metal construction. From this stile go up the field with the hedge on the left to another stile and then head diagonally across the next field to the far corner. *Offa's Dyke can be seen clearly by the line of trees across the next field to the left.* Bear right through a small belt of trees and then bear left again to a stile which leads out onto a road. Turn left along this ignoring the waymarked track ahead and continue to climb for about half a mile.

At a crossroads by the corner of Wern [Alder Swamp] Wood a road going off to the right is a short cut up to Fron Isaf [Lower Hillside]. To get views of Chirk (see Walk 12) in the valley on the left continue ahead, passing Fron [Hillside] Cottage. Unfortunately the most prominent features of Chirk are factories on the outskirts.

2. Where a road with a better surface comes in from the right turn back on it. *(The ODP continues along the road ahead, joining Walk 12 in about 150 yards.)* The road climbs (and the view to the right improves as a result) to the junction in Fron Isaf. Bear left here by the telephone box and in about 100 yards turn right onto a track which descends between large sycamore trees. When the track bends right go ahead through a gate to the bottom edge of a wood.

There is now a good view of part of the Dee Valley and the railway viaduct across it below to the right.

Go left through the hedgeline at a gate and turn right to follow it before going down towards a projecting section of Fron Wood. *The Vale of Llangollen can now be seen to the left.*

From the wood corner bear right towards another wood, entering it over a stile about 20 yards to the left of a gate into the next field. Follow the path in the wood until it reaches a track and turn right along this through a fine wood. Look out for a path on the left when it has nearly reached the A5 and take this down to the footway beside the road. Turn left to return to the start of the walk, passing St David's Church, the Post Office and the Britannia Inn.

Chirk

This is basically a walk round the outside of the grounds of Chirk Castle, which is seen from time to time. The latter part is alongside the River Ceiriog, passing under aqueduct and viaduct.

Distance: *6¾ miles.*

Start: *In Chirk at the junction of the main street and Station Avenue. Grid ref: 291 377 (Landranger 126, Pathfinder 827). Parking is available behind the British Legion building, being reached via Colliery Road, which is across from Station Avenue somewhat towards Wrexham.*

By bus: *Midland Red North (Oswestry) run the 2/2A service between Wrexham and Oswestry, Tanat Valley Coaches have the D60 between Oswestry and Llanarmon D.C. and Bryn Melyn have the D95 (Weds and Sats) from Llangollen to Oswestry. In all cases alight at the Hand Hotel.*

By train: *Chirk is on the line from Chester to Shrewsbury. The station is passed soon after the start of the walk.*

Now that the A5 bypasses it Chirk is a pleasant, quiet place. The centre is small, grouped round the church, which is mainly 15th century although there are traces of Norman work, and the Hand Hotel, but there are extensive housing estates to the north and some industry. The most famous features, Chirk Castle and the Telford canal aqueduct are outside the town.

The town's history goes back a long way. The Normans built a castle here and another nearby. The town apparently takes its name from the River Ceiriog. There is doubt about the meaning of this. Some people say that it means "abounding in trout", but George Borrow, who visited the town in the course of his journey through "Wild Wales", reckoned that it was derived from "cerrig", a rock. In the 15th century Chirk was a place of note with a "Great Hall".

*Henry II granted the town a special charter exempting its inhabitants from the law preventing Welshmen from owning property in English towns. About this time too, occurred the event possibly leading to the Red Hand (as at the hotel) becoming the local motif, as the Welsh for murderer is literally "red hand". The vicar of Llanvrothen adopted the son of Ieuan ap Robert, to the disgust of a larger landowner (and the possessor of a longer name!), Howell ap Rhys ap Howell Vaughan, who felt that **his** son should have been chosen for this honour. Two of Howell's brothers murdered the priest and one fled to Chirk, where he was apprehended. Ieuan ap Robert supervised the beheading, but his chosen axeman was so inefficient that the murderer objected and Ieuan finished the job himself in a rage! The red hand is also the symbol of baronetcy of the Myddleton family of Chirk Castle.*

Robert, Earl of Dudley, was granted the Lordship of Chirk in 1563, in exchange for that of Skipton. Since then the town has declined gently until recent industrial development has led to something of a revival.

The Route

1. Start along Station Avenue, by the War Memorial and the gates into the recreation ground which (on a much smaller scale) keep up the tradition at Chirk Castle. *"Avenue" refers to the lime trees, which presumably were once on both sides of the road.* Pass the entrance to the Cadbury's works and the station entrance and cross bridges over the railway and, as it emerges from a tunnel, the Llangollen branch of the Shropshire Union Canal. Just beyond this it is possible to take a path on the right into a strip of woodland and later, before a "Private" sign, turn left to a stile and walk across a field to rejoin the road. However, this by-passes the magnificent wrought iron gates at the entrance to Chirk Castle.

The gates were made near Wrexham in the early 1700s, and are amazing for the delicacy of the work and the complexity of the design, which is topped by a pair of wolves (the emblem of the Myddleton family) made in lead and the Myddleton shield.

Turn right by the gates and follow the road for about half a mile, passing a golf course in the latter stages. Pass under a beautiful spreading oak tree and bear left. Just after two more

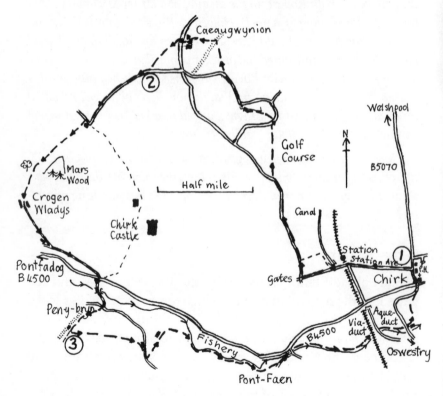

Walking down into the Ceiriog valley

fine oaks on the right go up a bank on the right to a stile by a footpath sign. Once over the stile keep to the fence on the right, with the golf course beyond it. *A good deal of new housing can be seen over to the right below a green ridge.* A stile leads into the next field. Go across this parallel to the fence on the right to reach another stile, which leads out into a lane.

Cross to a stile opposite on the bend, head left to a protruding corner of a fence and then continue with the fence on the right. *Rabbits and pheasants may well be scurrying into the rough ground across the fence.* Shortly before the field corner take a stile on the right and cross the stream by a little stone bridge. Turn left to a stile onto another road. Go up the hedged track ahead, which has two strips of tarmac. Bend to the left with it, but when it turns sharply to the left go ahead over a stile. Keep to the hedge on the right until it reaches the bank of Offa's Dyke, slanting across from the left.

Go over a stile and left up a fenced track to the farm of Caeaugwynion [White fields]. At the farm turn left, then right after a few yards through an arch in the barns, where there is a waymark. Bear left through the yard and turn right just before the house to the road. Turn right along this for about 25 yards to a fingerpost. *(To link up with Walk 11 it is necessary to go ahead here for about 200 yards to a road junction.)* Go up the track on the left and immediately over a stile on the left. Cross the field, keeping to the left of the highest point to find a stile in the corner of the field. Bear a bit more to the left in this field to another stile which leads onto a road.

2. Turn right here.

Chirk Castle can be seen over to the left when it is not hidden behind clumps of trees. Now in the care of the National Trust, the castle has a very uncompromising exterior dating from the fourteenth century, when it was built as part of Edward I's attempt to conquer Wales. It changed hands several times during and after the Civil War, when it was much damaged. Since 1595, the Myddleton family have lived here and have made the interior much more comfortable! In the summer months a waymarked alternative route goes through the park, starting from where the road bends right.

To follow the official route of the ODP, bend right with the road, but turn left over a stile almost immediately. Follow a track which winds up the field and through a gateway. Now grassy, the track keeps to the right of a plantation of conifers (Mars Wood). Just over the crest of the hill go through a gate or over the fence beside it and slant down on the track further to the left. *Soon the valley of the River Ceiriog is seen ahead.* Pass to the left of a section of wall. The track turns left to a gate, but the ODP goes ahead over a stile, only to turn left to rejoin the track. Soon pass between the buildings of Crogen Wladys [Gladys's Gill] farm and continue to descend into the valley of the River Ceiriog, which can be heard gurgling below. Pass above another house, with a complicated roof structure and bear left along the lane, eventually reaching the B4500.

In the narrow valley here is Castle Mill. It is thought that Crogen Castle once stood here. It was another Norman fortress, and was the site of the Battle of Crogen, between Henry II and a Welsh force including Owain Gwynedd and Cadwalader.

Cross the B4500 to a road which soon crosses the river and climbs up, entering Shropshire in the process, to another road at Pen-y-bryn [Hilltop]. *The road to the left cuts out some climbing and possibly muddy paths, but it also misses the best views across the valley to Chirk Castle. The Maelor Way begins along this road, on the start of its task to link the ODP with the Sandstone Trail and Shropshire Way at Grindley Brook.*

Chirk Castle seen across the Ceiriog Valley

Go ahead, still with the ODP, up an enclosed path between houses and cottages. Be careful to keep right where indicated. The vehicle ruts above here may be drier than the bits between. Cross a miry cow track, with stiles each side. *The line of trees on the right marks Offa's Dyke again.* Go up from the track to the corner of a hedge and then follow it up. *Looking back now Chirk Castle stands out very well above a band of trees.* Go over a stile beside Gibralta (sic) Cottage, which backs onto the dyke.

3. Turn left and proceed with a fence on the left. The farmer here believes in electric fences and it may be necessary to unlatch one to get out of the field. Go ahead above an old quarry, now taken over by trees. Go ahead along the track and over the stile beside a gate. Bear left to a climbable bit of fence in the hedge and from this to a gate which leads out onto a lane. Cross this to a stile slightly to the left. Cross the field and go through the next hedgeline, then bear left through another hedgeline before turning right along it. Go over a stile beside a gate and along a grassy track beside a building which is an old school, to come out onto the road again.

Go right for a short distance, then turn down a track on the left, with the distinctive Maelor Way arrow (which is apparently made up of the letters M and W). Keep on down, ignoring drives to right and left, and, at a whitewashed cottage, go ahead through three gates onto an enclosed path. At the end of the path go over a stile into a small field and turn right onto an obvious path to another stile leading into woodland. The path climbs, up steps to the right at one point, with the many pools of the Chirk Fishery below across the River Ceiriog, and then descends steeply to the river bank. Cross a ditch to a stile where another path goes right. In the long pasture keep close to the river bank, going over a stream and cutting through a ridge in the process. From the ridge the path goes further away from the river, with the buildings of Pont-Faen [Stonebridge] up to the right. A grassy track leads to a stile beside a gate. Continue ahead, along the narrow road from Pont-Faen to Pont-faen Bridge.

Go over the bridge (leaving the Maelor Way and re-entering Wrexham) and then go right over a stile, now with a waymark of a red hand (like the sign of the hotel in Chirk). Resume the riverside walk through another pasture, now with the river on the right. In front are the railway viaduct and, behind it, the aqueduct of the Llangollen branch of the Shropshire Union Canal, which was built by Thomas Telford in 1795. There are stiles either side of the viaducts and then another pasture. At the end of this the river goes under Chirk Bridge, which carries the road formerly known as the A5, but the path goes up a slope to the road. *A sign indicates that the other side of the bridge is in Shropshire.*

Cross the road (more easily than before the new road was built to the east) and take a track to the left of the entrance to Seventh Heaven Antique Beds. A track, tarmacked at first, leads to a robust fence which has to be climbed, and the path zigzags over a mill leat. Go along the leat for a while and then branch right up and across the field.

This field has many ridges, probably defences for the motte (a mound, especially with a castle) which was once where the new houses are, behind the wall at the top of the hill. (There was another motte across the valley, presumably the two guarded a strategically important point.) Looking back it is obvious that the "antique beds" building was once a watermill. The new A5 can also be seen crossing the Ceiriog.

Go over a stile in the hedge to the left of the wall onto the road and turn right, passing the parish church (which has fine monuments of the Myddleton and Trevor families), to return to the start of the walk.

Selattyn

The walk goes over Selattyn Hill and includes pleasant undulating farmland with views across Shropshire and a fine
stretch of the Offa's Dyke Path, with good examples of the
Dyke itself.

Distance: *6¼ miles.*

Start: *Start in Selattyn, which is about two miles west of the A5 and
can be reached from the east via Weston Rhyn or Gobowen. Safe parking spots can be found in the village with care. Grid ref: 266 340
(Landranger 126, Pathfinder 827).*

By bus: *There is no service to Selattyn. For services to Racecourse
Hill (point 3) see walk 14, but check if there is enough time available
to do the walk at your usual pace.*

*Selattyn [Oak village by a gully, or settlement of the ploughs or gullies]
is a pleasant village, clustered round the church of St Mary the Virgin
and the Cross Keys pub. The church apparently has fine roofs, but as it
is not normally open all that can be admired are the stepped tower of
1704, topped by a cockerel windvane, and the double-headed grave-
stones in the churchyard.*

The Route

1. Start down a track with the church lych gate and the postbox
on the right, passing a number of cottages. Keep right at the
entrance to Yew Tree Cottage, now on a grassy track. Cross a

stream by a stone bridge with wooden parapets and turn right with the hedge. Climb with a hedge, initially intermittent, on the right. *Back across the valley, the church stands out well.* Climb a fence beside a gate to reach a road. Turn right and climb gently for nearly half a mile, with the valley of the Morlas Brook below to the right.

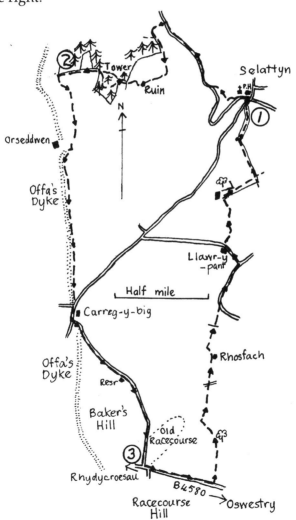

Turn left up a rough track. Follow the track round to the left but, when it goes right, go ahead on a grassy path (signposted to Selattyn Hill) with a fence on the left.

Fine views develop to the left over the Shropshire Plain. When Selattyn comes into view below, Gobowen is beyond it to the left, with Weston Rhyn and Chirk (with its industry) further to the left.

Climb an old gate (unless it has been replaced by something better) and continue with the fence on the left. It appears as though the path has once been between walls, and this continues after turning right at another ruined wall. The path now climbs with a large coniferous plantation over to the right.

Unless a stile has been put in the crossing wall, go through a gate towards a ruined building and then turn right through another gate to resume the climb, now with a stout stone wall on the left. Follow the wall round to the right and left and then go over a stile into another field. Continue up with the wood immediately on the right to another stile, which leads into the wood.

There is a seat here, with a fine view southeast over Shropshire, with Oswestry round to the right. When I first came up here, in November 1997, the wood was completely impenetrable but co-operation between the landowner, Shropshire and volunteer labour has produced a choice of two routes.

The broad way has been cleared through the bracken round to the left. The narrow way goes between the trees ahead but is easy to follow. About half way it passes to the left of a ruin. *This is the remains of Selattyn Tower, which was erected by a clergyman to commemorate a battle between the Saxons and the British.* Unlike their biblical precedents the broad and narrow ways converge at a stile, where a fingerpost points the way towards Offa's Dyke.

Go over the stile and keep along the right edge of the sheep pasture, with the wood adjacent on the right, except where there is an inlet of pasture further along. *From the top of the rise the line of Offa's Dyke can be picked out, going down to the left and passing between two blocks of woodland. It will be seen more closely later.* When there is a stile ahead the Offa's Dyke Path (ODP) is joined by turning left before the stile.

2. Go down the grassy track, bearing left when the fence turns right and then right past a stile, from which the ODP is a footpath between banks of bracken. There are fences first on the left and then, after a ruin, on the right. After a gate and stile the ODP turns right along a track. Go over a stile or a cattle grid near Orseddwen [White Barrow] farm and turn left to a stile. *Remains which were found when the nearby barrow was excavated may have been of one Gwên, killed in a battle in 540.* Cross a stream by a wooden bridge and go up steps to a stile. *Offa's Dyke is just to the right of the path, soon in fine shape with a ditch over on the other side of the bank. We spend about a mile in its company now.*

Before long there are woods, first on the right and then, with the path in its edge, on the left. *The trees are mainly conifers, with a few token deciduous trees at the edge to soften the outline of the solid blocks.* A path from the right breaks through the Dyke and the ODP crosses a marshy stream on planks. Eventually another stile (on the Wales—England border and giving distances to Prestatyn and Chepstow) leads onto a road at Carreg-y-big [Brow of the stone] farm, which is also the Oswestry Equestrian Centre.

Turn right and then twice left to pass the farm and go along the road to "Old Racecourse and Oswestry". Offa's Dyke leaves the ODP to go over Baker's Hill, where the ODP was not allowed to follow. As we climb the hill the Dyke can be seen slanting away to the right. The road passes an unexpected Severn Trent reservoir at the top of the hill and bears right in two places. Soon after the second, beyond houses on the left, there are traces of the old Oswestry Race Course. The part parallel to the road makes good springy walking on the turf.

Church of St Mary the Virgin, Selattyn

The racecourse was in operation possibly from 1728 to 1848. Unusually its shape was a figure of eight, with the crossover where the B4580 now runs. The site is now common land and a very popular amenity.

Soon we come to the B4580. *(Walk 14 continues from this point up to the top of Racecourse Hill.)*

3. Take the B4580 to the left (signed to Oswestry) downhill for nearly half a mile. There is a good footway on the left. Pass a house on the left and a drive to another, which is set back in a field. Just past an elegant drive on the right take a stile on the left. From this go up the field with a hedge on the right.

A fine view over the Shropshire plain is developing over the hedge. The range of the Breidden Hills (see Walk 17) should be in sight looking to the left of the path down the hill, with Shrewsbury to the left of that. Much nearer at hand is Oswestry, just south of east, with the fort of Old Oswestry on a hill just to the north.

At the top of the hill two stiles in quick succession lead to the edge of a beech wood. From the second bear left across a rough field along a path which curves left through a hedge line and then aims for a stile hidden in the next hedge at the junction of blackthorn and gorse and about 30 yards to the right of a gate. Over the stile turn right on a stony track, passing a house and ignoring footpaths to left and right. The track descends and crosses a tarmacked lane. *The ground on the right appears to have been wooded, but now only communication masts remain.*

Bear left at Rhosfach [Little Moor] to a gate or stile. Through or over one of these turn left to another gate and stile about 25 yards away. Beyond these turn right with a line of trees on the right. *You may be besieged by pheasants along this stretch unless they have met the fate they were reared for in the nearby wood.* Go over a stile and keep the same line as far as possible steeply down through another deforested area. Go ahead on the lane which has come from the right and turn left at a junction with a sign to Crown House.

Continue past the farm of Llawr-y-pant [Floor-of-the-valley] and turn right over a stile by the second gate. The next stile is obvious across the field beyond what has been a well. From the stile keep to the left of the line of trees, watching out for rabbit holes. Go through a gateway into the next field, now with a hedge on the right. About 50 yards from the gate ahead turn right over a stile and aim for the corner of the wood to reach another stile. Continue from here in the same direction, slowly leaving the fence on the right with the air probably thick with the inhabitants of the rookery in the wood to the left.

Turn left along the crossing hedge/fence, go through a gate and pass a small pond. Just before the house ahead go over a stile on the right in the corner of the field and take a narrow path between hedges (a "green lane"). This leads down to a road where turning right brings you back to Selattyn.

Rhydycroesau

Over Racecourse Hill, then mainly on two ridges either side of the River Morda—Craig Forda, with Offa's Dyke and lovely woods, and Craig-y-Rhiw, which gives beautiful views into Wales.

Distance: *6 miles (or 4¾ if —as recommended—the bus is used from Rhydycroesau to Racecourse Hill).*

Start: *In Rhydycroesau by the village hall, on the B4580 at the east end of the village. There is parking space on the road as well as by the hall. Grid ref: 242 308 (Landranger 126, Pathfinder 827 - 847 also needed for walk). If starting to walk at Racecourse Hill (point 2) the grid ref: is 258 310.*

By bus: *There is a service through the village between Oswestry and LLansilin via Racecourse Hill on Wednesdays, Saturdays and schooldays only. The service number is 455, operated by Midland Red North (Oswestry) and Tanat Valley Coaches. (Make sure that there is enough time to do the walk at your usual pace.) Alight at the village hall or at Racecourse Hill.*

Rhydycroesau [Ford of the crossings] is a hamlet, nestling beside the bridge over the River Cynllaith [Grass or Slaughter]. In view of its small size it must draw on a wide area to fill the church and the village hall (which houses a recent, prizewinning tapestry map of the village). There is also a Post Office and stores (open Thursday morning and Wednesday only) but no pub. The bridge, which replaced an earlier one, was built in 1818. Christ Church was built in 1838 and renovated in 1886.

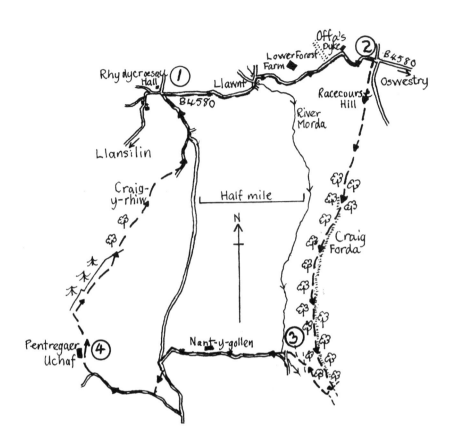

The Route

1. There is no worthwhile alternative to walking along the B5480 to Racecourse Hill, so it is recommended that the bus be used if possible. Those who are walking should follow the road to and through the scattered hamlet of Llawnt [Lawn or glade].

The Cross Foxes Inn dates back at least to the 1830's, when the bridge was rebuilt. It once had a reputation for riotous behaviour.

Ignore two turns to the left and start the climb up to the ridge of Racecourse Hill, crossing the River Morda.

*On the way up there is a good view down the valley of the River
Morda to the right, below Racecourse Hill and the woods on the sand-
stone ridge of Craig Forda. [Morda and Forda have the same mean-
ing—Great Taf, where Taf, a common river name, may mean Dark
River.] Further up Offa's Dyke can be seen to the left on its way over
Baker's Hill, crossing the road midway between Lower Forest Farm
and the first of three sharp bends in the last stages of the climb up to
Racecourse Hill.*

2. At the crest of the hill turn right just before the road on the
right to Trefonen and Treflach. *Walk 13 comes from the left and
continues along the B5480 from here. Something of the history of Racecourse Hill is given in the description of that walk.*

Take the path waymarked with the Offa's Dyke Path (ODP)
acorn (parallel to the road to Trefonen and Treflach) over the
short grass of the old racecourse up to the top of the hill, where
there are benches and fine diagrams of the scenery to west and
south.

*The only snag with these diagrams is that the views can hardly be
seen because of trees which have presumably grown since the Rotary
Club of Oswestry installed the diagrams. Mynydd Lledrod [Slippery
Mountain] can be seen to the west, but little else. (There is a more
useful diagram of the country to the east in the car park down on that
side of the hill.)*

Continue ahead, passing to the right of a stylised stone sculpture with a horse's head at each end and a saddle (just the right
size for two small children).

Follow ODP waymarking into Racecourse Wood. Keep
straight on, ignoring a path to the left. Leave Racecourse Wood
at a stile and descend with a fence on the left and bracken on
the right. Enter woodland which is initially scrubby but soon
becomes delightful along the ridge of Craig Forda [Great Taf
Ridge]. As indicated by the waymarks turn right and left in
quick succession past a gate, crossing the mound of Offa's Dyke,

onto a track which is initially broad and hard, but also has sections which are not so. *The Dyke continues as a mound to the left, often with trees growing through it—showing no respect for an ancient monument.* Pass through a fine stand of taller trees on a good section of path. *The valley below to the right is that of the River Morda.*

On the left may be noticed a stone semicircle with uncomfortable-looking seats. (There has been a previous one which was in disrepair.) Ignore a path branching left. Take the track ahead to pass to the right of a stony knoll and pass another semicircular stone seat. Fork left where another ride forks right and turn right at a track

Viewpoint sculpture on Racecourse Hill

crossing. Follow the waymarks left down the slope to another T-junction. The ODP turns left here but we go straight on. Keep straight on at the first crossing with the ground sloping down to the left. Go ahead down a steep path at the next junction in an area where horse chestnuts and then beech seem to be the predominant trees. Go left at the next junction and pass a partly ivy-covered ruin down on the left.

3. Go ahead over a lane to a footbridge across the River Morda. Across the river bear left and then right up a hedged track which once forded the river. This leads up to a road which is surfaced even though, apparently, it is unsuitable for vehicles. Go up this, quite steeply at first, for about half a mile, passing the farm of Nant-y-gollen [Hazel gorge] midway. The road bends left sharply soon before a T-junction.

Turn left here and turn in through a gate on the right in about 100 yards. Keep as close as practical to the hedge on the right up the field, at the top going through gates to reach a road. Turn right here to a junction where our route goes right over a cattle grid. Follow the track to Pentregaer Uchaf [Upper Camp Village] farm. *(The site of the camp is on the hill above the farm)*.

4. Keep to the right of all the buildings, with gates and stiles before and after them. Continue with a hedge on the right, but from the end of the tennis court beyond it bear left up the field. This should lead to a stile in the far corner. From this aim for a projecting corner of the coniferous wood which covers the first part of the steep limestone slope down from Craig-y-rhiw [Hill Ridge]. *(If you have been hearing gunfire, this will probably have been from the range at the foot of the slope.)* Continue along the edge of the wood, but try not to miss a lovely view back to the right through the gap above Tyn-y-coed. After two more stiles in quick succession the trees on the slope are deciduous and scattered, so the views over Wales (which starts at the bottom of the slope) are splendid.

It is unfortunate that the view diagrams are not here rather than on Racecourse Hill. The river Cynllaith comes down a lovely valley to the northwest, passes below the escarpment and heads southwest towards the hills across the Tanat valley. In between the Afon Ogau [River Harrows] also heads northwest between Mynydd Lledrod (to the right) and Gyrn Moelfre [Bald Hill with Horns], over whose northern shoulder the Berwyn Mountains may be seen on a clear day.

Keep to the edge of the escarpment, crossing a broken wall, to a stile beside a broken gate. Continue down a shallow valley, getting a view ahead to the old racecourse and Baker's Hill and down to the left to Rhydycroesau. After a gateway the path bears right to hummocky ground—the remains of quarrying. A stile in the wall beside a gate leads out into a rather muddy lane. Turn left down this, avoiding the mud as much as possible, to reach a gate which leads out onto a road. Turn left and descend to the start.

Trefonen and Nantmawr

Through pleasant undulating countryside with fine views (weather permitting) from Moelydd and plenty of interest.

Distance: *6 miles.*

Start: *Begin in Trefonen, at the junction of the road from Oswestry and Bellan Lane. This is very much the centre of the village, with two public houses. Apart from their car parks the best place to park is probably along Bellan Lane when it widens out, but the road opposite, School Lane, has plenty of space and leads to the village hall, with its own car park. Grid ref: 260 268 (Landranger 126, Pathfinder 847).*

By bus: *Trefonen is served by the D54 between Bryn and Oswestry (Midland Red, Oswestry).*

In 1272 the township of Trefonen [Birch town] was "obliged to keep the lord's hounds" according to a contemporary document. In the 19th century it was a minor centre of coal mining. The village of Trefonen has recently expanded a great deal. Whether the two pubs, the Barley Mow and the Efel [Tongs] Inn are the cause or effect of this, who can say? The church, built in 1821 "for Welsh speaking people", is along the Oswestry road.

The Route

1. Go along Bellan Lane joining the Offa's Dyke Path (ODP) en-route. When the lane bends right continue ahead down a track to a stile into a field. Go ahead, with the hedge on the right sparse at first but soon more substantial. From the stile at the end of the field bear left over a stream and then continue with a hedge on the left to another stile. Go up the field, keeping to the left of trees and then bear more to the left to a stile which leads onto a road.

Turn left and then very soon right along a side road. When this splits go right and then bend round to the left at Ty Canol [Middle House]. As you continue up the track spare a look behind. *The nearest hill is Mynydd Myfyr [Contemplation Mountain], formed of Cefn sandstone.* This is a pleasant stretch, with rock outcrops among the trees on the left and farmland beyond the fence on the right. Leave the track by climbing a stile to the right of two gates and go up the field with a hedge on the right. Turn left in the field corner near the farm of Moelydd Uchaf [Upper Hills]. (Moelydd is the hill we are starting to climb). Keep to the hedge on the right and follow it round to the right, now on a stony track. Go over a stile beside another gate and turn right, still with the track. Leave this when it goes left and take the grassy path up through bracken and gorse to the top of Moelydd.

The top is marked by a square plinth round a metal pole which may be a flagpole on occasions. On a clear day there are magnificent views all round from here. Mynydd Myfyr is to the north, Oswestry to the NE, the Shropshire plain from there round to Llanymynech [Monk's Church] Hill with the Breidden Hills beyond to the SE. The River Tanat crosses from SW to South in its valley to flow into the Vyrnwy. Mynydd y Bryn [Hill Mountain] is NW, with the Berwyns behind.

Leave Moelydd just to the right of the way up, keeping above the bracken until the waymarked route down through it is seen.

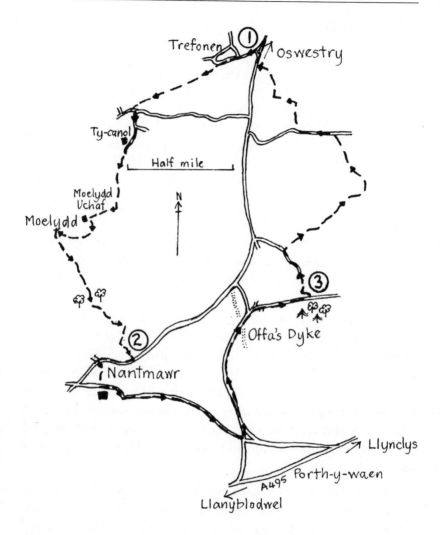

Bear left into a track which passes above an extended cottage which is surrounded by a fine selection of birds and animals. When the track bears left continue with the fence on the right, noting one of the original concrete ODP markers, now a rarity. Bear right with the hedge to a stile then bear left between haw-thorn bushes to a stile leading into the Jones' Rough Nature

Reserve. The path goes down through this quite clearly through the coppice to another stile. Over this turn left on another track, the surface of which soon improves. Continue ahead at a junction then watch out for a stile in the right hand hedge. Go down the field from here towards Nantmawr [Great Valley] with a hedge on the left in which the next stile is hidden. The path from this slants down to go over a stile to the right of the prominent house. An enclosed path leads down to a road in Nantmawr.

Nantmawr was once a major centre for limestone quarrying. The "Potteries" goods line was in operation from 1866 to 1966, with up to 2000 tons per year being moved out through Llanymynech (see Walk 16). Now it has a quiet air, but there are traces of the quarrying and railway still to be seen.

2. Turn right here down through the village to a bridge over a stream then up again to turn left over a stile opposite a road on the right. Go up through the wood to another stile into a field. Go left to join a hedge on the left and follow this up to a stile beside a gate. Go out onto the road near Cefn [Ridge] Farm and turn left to descend gradually for about ¾ mile.

Over to the left can be seen scars from quarry workings and, in the valley, the buttressed construction for loading stone onto rail wagons, now partially overgrown. The track of the railway, which is crossed, is now a mass of saplings. The scattered buildings of Porth-y-Waen [Meadow Gate] are seen ahead.

Turn left at a crossroads to go uphill on a wider road.

There are a number of houses on the right, perched up above the road to get full benefit of the view to Nantmawr and Moelydd among other things. On the left, Ty Gwyn [White House] is even better placed. The next bungalow on the right is called Bryn Offa [Offa Hill] in recognition of the section of Offa's Dyke immediately beyond it, going back round the hillside. The continuation across the road is obvious through the field below.

Fork right on a minor road, Wern y Weil. Continue along this until about 100 yards after a wood starts on the right.

3. Turn left up a track and in 30 yards turn left on a grassy track. Soon take a path forking up to the right. Where a right fork leads to a gate, fork left. Pass a rather splendid new house which belies its name of Peartree **Cottage** and join the drive from it. Go left at the next junction and pass a farm track on the left.

Turn in through the next gate on the right or climb the fence beside it and head rightish to a climbable fence at the bottom of the field. Aim for a cattle crossing in the next hedge and then go up the hill with a hedge on the right. At the end of the field go over another fence then descend with a hedge on the right. *The strip of woodland running parallel across the field to the right glories in the name of Big Bellan Covert.* Climb the fence beside the gate at the bottom of the field and go ahead onto a path slanting up to the right, to the bottom of an oak plantation on the skyline. With a wire fence on the right, pass through a gate, ignore a gate on the right and continue near the hedge on the right (with a new bungalow in the field below) as far as the next gate on the right.

Bear diagonally left here past the power line pole and continue to a two-bar stile in the next hedge. Continue in the same line diagonally across the next field, climbing a bank, to reach a gate and stile leading out into a lane. Turn left until level with the second house on the left. Go in through the first of two adjacent gates on the right. Climb with a hedge on the left to a group of trees on the top of the hill. Just past these go left through a gate and then down the hill with a hedge on the right. At the next crossing hedge turn right through a gate and go along the hedge on the left for about 40 yards. Climb the fence on the left and bear down right. Once over the crest of the hill a waymarked stile can be seen ahead. Go over this and bear diagonally left

Trefonen

towards the stream on the right to find a stone footbridge and stile. Over these, bear left into a paddock and leave this at the opposite corner, over the fence. Turn right here to get to the start of the walk.

Llanymynech

This walk is in two loops. The northern loop winds its way up onto Llanymynech Hill with fine views along the Severn Valley. The southern is on a canal towpath with the return (best avoided by using the bus) along the A483.

Distance: *The northern loop is 3¼ miles, the southern 3½. The latter can be reduced by a mile by using the bus (see details below) instead of the unpleasant walk along the A483. (It is possible to park near Llandysilio church, grid ref: 268 194, to do the bus journey first.)*

Start: *Start at the main crossroads in Llanymynech, where the A483 and the B4398 cross. There is a car park off the B4398 heading westwards. Grid ref: 267 209 (Landranger 126, Pathfinder 847 - 868 also needed for the southern loop).*

By bus: *Llanymynech is served by the D71 service between Oswestry and Welshpool, which also passes Llandysilio church (Midland Red North, Oswestry) and by the 445 between Llanfyllin and Oswestry (Tanat Valley Coaches).*

Considering its small village status today, Llanymynech [Monk's (or, possibly, Mines') Church] has a surprising history, all stemming from Llanymynech Hill to the north. It was mined for copper in the Bronze Age and the Romans mined for various minerals, but the boom time began in the late 18th century with quarrying of the limestone hill, mainly for the production of quicklime for "sweetening" fields. This led to the canal being built, initially as a spur from the Shropshire Union Canal at Welsh Frankton. Later the canal was extended southwards, but it never achieved the planned links with the Mersey and the navigable section of the Severn. The stone was transported in barges but had to be processed after unloading as the combination of quicklime, wooden hulls and water would have been disastrous. As a result there were limekilns at intervals along the canals.

Later the canal was superseded by the railways and five lines radiated from Llanymynech, all now dismantled. The industrial history is best studied on the trails which start off the A483 just to the north of the canal. The A483 through Llanymynech is along the line of Offa's Dyke.

The church is an interesting curiosity. Its dedication is unusual for a start, as it is one of only five "St Agatha's" in England and Wales. The church is in the diocese of Lichfield but parts of the parish are in England and parts in Wales. Built in 1844, the church is in the "Normanesque" style and looks as though it would be more at home by a piazza near the Mediterranean. Although the stone is local much of the decoration is in terra cotta. Inside the integrity of the plan has been preserved by banishing monuments from the previous church to the back. Brass plates from the 18th century are behind the medieval font and stone ones (as old as 1692) up in the gallery, which is reached past the mechanism of the clock. This produces some amazing noises, particularly as it prepares to strike.

Just north of the church is the Red Lion, which straddles the Wales/England border. This was a distinct advantage when Wales was "dry" on Sundays!

The Route

1. Walk south along the A483 towards Welshpool. Turn left along the lane between the Red Lion and the church. The lane bends right, left and left again (at The Old Rectory) to reach the B4398. Cross this to a footpath sign to the right of the hall opposite.

This indicates the right of way across the playground and sports field, but it is inadvisable to take the direct route if a game of football is in progress! Cross the stile in the far corner of the field and walk with the hedge on the right to another stile, which gives access to a towpath beside the defunct Montgomeryshire Canal.

The tall chimney across the canal belongs to a Hoffman Horizontal Ring Limekiln. This enabled limestone to be processed in a more or less continuous fashion and more economically, by sections of the kiln being loaded on a daily basis, so that various sections were "cooking" at different stages together. The kiln operated only from 1889 to 1914, as its introduction coincided with the replacement of quicklime for concrete, chemical and agricultural production. The kiln, with its catacomb-like interior, is well worth a visit by anyone with an interest in industrial archaeology.

Turn right along the towpath. Continue between the piers of an old railway bridge. *(There is a board across the canal, giving historic information about the railways.)* The remains of the canal diverge from those of a railway, with an unusually well landscaped sewage works and a field used for showjumping in between. When houses are reached on both sides of the canal go under the bridge and then turn back over it along a road. The road leads up past a garden which appears to be supported by a line of limekilns. Keep climbing to the A483, ignoring a level road to the left. *(If you have found the climb a struggle you may be interested to know that you have got to Pant [Hollow].)*

2. Cross the road with care, slanting right, and go up the track past the Methodist Church. Go through a wooden kissing gate onto an enclosed path past a sports ground. Beyond another kissing gate the path continues through a tunnel of vegetation. Where paths cross near an iron fence go ahead over a stile and then bear right round the angle of the fence passing one stile to a second across the path.

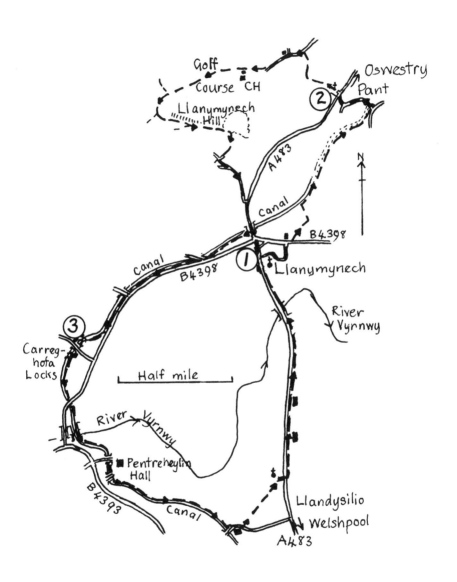

The trees to the left are festooned with Clematis Vitalba, which starts its year as Traveller's Joy and finishes it as Old Man's Beard.

Cross the stile, continue along and up with houses below to the right and pass two houses on the left. A stile leads onto a track which in turn leads to a lane. Turn left here up the hill and left again, still uphill, at Haulfryn [Sunhill] The High. This leads onto the golf course.

The golf course is riddled with holes from mining back to Roman times, which must be a problem if the golfers hit those instead of the little ones with flags in! Rights of way across the course are clearly indicated, which gives golfers no excuse for strafing you, but it is still advisable to use discretion.

Head to the right of the clubhouse, which is on a hummock ahead, pass the garages and continue ahead as indicated by the bridleway sign. Go just to the right of a green to another marker post and then bear left up a surfaced track. Go over the crest of the hill and pass the 18th tee. On the descent pass to the left of another green and then turn left at a finger post, now with the Offa's Dyke Path (ODP). The path goes through a gate and then through scrubland with blackthorn, just below the edge of the plateau in a Montgomeryshire Wildlife Trust nature reserve.

As the path comes round a corner below Asterley Rocks a view opens up to the south over Llanymynech, with the Breidden Hills behind. [Breidden may mean "walled town on a hill", but I have also seen Craig Breidden translated as Brython's Rock.] This is an area where the wild roses are white with flowers in the summer and red with hips in the autumn. It is encouraging how beautifully nature has reclaimed what must have been a scene of dereliction.

The path descends clearly if roughly at times and goes to the right of a huge amphitheatre quarried out of the hill. A stile leads into England and the descent is steeper through a hazel copse but levels off with a turn to the right. The second of two stiles gives access to a lane which leads down to a crossroads by a postbox where the only collection is at 7am. Turn left and follow the road down to the A483. Turn right.

Carreghofa Locks on the Montgomery Canal

1. (again) If the southern loop is to be done at once cross over to the other side of the road. Pass over the canal and then turn down left and go back under the road.

This stretch of the canal has not yet been returned to a navigable state, as can be seen from the trees growing in and across it, but there is water in most of it. One exception to this is where Carreghofa Lane crosses over it. Presumably this once went over the now redundant bridge. The ODP continues along the towpath.

The B4398 is just beyond the hedgerow on the left. In summer this hedgerow and the canal bank are full of flowers and the air is rich with butterflies, dragonflies and damselflies. Swans, mallards, coots and moorhens are the birds most likely to be seen on the water.

The canal bears round to the left and the wooded Bryn Mawr [Big Hill], which is topped by an ancient fort, is seen ahead. The B4398 is left when the canal bears right to Carreghofa [Hanging stone] Locks.

3. *This is a lovely spot in summer, with a lock each side of a bridge, and old toll and lock-keeper's cottages and a wharfinger's house (which is now let for holidays). An information board gives the history, including disputes between the owners of the two canals which met here. A little further on the BBC filmed an episode of Our Mutual Friend recently.*

The canal turns back to cross the B4398 which is at canal level. *(These crossings will cause problems if the plan to reopen the canal ever comes to fruition.)* Soon the canal passes over the River Vyrnwy on an aqueduct. [More accurately Efyrnwy, the Vyrnwy is a head river of the Severn, and so shares its name in an altered form.] There are bridges over the canal either side of Pentreheylin Hall, which is seen below on the left. The canal meanders gently for the next half mile with the Vyrnwy in sight across fields to the left.

Just before a bridge with wooden fences, the ODP turns off to the left, passes a farm and goes down a lane. This leads to the A483, but it is possible to take a short cut to Llandysilio [Church of St Tysilio] church. Just after a gate on the left a climbable fence gives access to a field across which the way is clear. Aim slightly to the right of the buildings near the church to reach a gate which leads into the lane between church and A483. Unless you are catching the bus to Llanymynech or are prepared to retrace your route along the canal, there is no real alternative to turning left along the A483. This is a very busy road and it will probably be necessary to walk almost continuously on the right hand verge. *There are a couple of farms by the road to relieve the monotony but the most interesting feature is Llanymynech Hill with the impressive cliffs left by the quarrying.* Shortly before re-entering Llanymynech the Vyrnwy is crossed again.

Tirymynach and the Severn

A largely level walk, much of it beside the River Severn, with good views of the Breidden Hills.

Distance: *6¾ miles (with an extra 2½ if from the B4392).*

Start: *Begin about two miles south of Ardd-lin on the A483 road between Oswestry and Welshpool. There is limited space for parking along the road signposted to Wern. (More if the layby has been re-opened). Grid ref: 261 133 (Landranger 126, Pathfinder 868).*

By bus: *There is only a very limited service along this road, the S4 run by Tanat Valley Coaches, which runs from Pentrefelin to Newtown to serve the Coleg Powys there. There is a much better service along the B4392. This is the D71 between Welshpool and Oswestry, run by Midland Red North (Oswestry). Alight at Varchoel Bridge, the stop for Burgedin Hall. (Grid ref: 243 137) Walk down the lane signposted to Wern [Alder Swamp] for about 1¼ miles, turning right at a junction after about ¼ mile.*

Tirymynach [Monk's land] gets its name from having belonged to the demolished monastery of Strata Marcella Abbey two miles to the south.

The Route

1. Start off along the lane on the east of the A483 (across from the one signposted to Wern). This is followed for about 1½ miles as it weaves about, linking a number of farms. Of these The

Maesydd [Fields], surrounded by a good mixture of trees, is the biggest.

On the stretch which passes The Maesydd it should be possible, on a clear day, to see a number of hills in the northwest sector. Most prominent, almost directly ahead, is Llanymynech [Monks' Church] Hill (see Walk 16). To the left of it could be Gyrn Moelfre [Bald Hill with Horns], and further round to the left, approximately northwest, the mass of the Berwyn Mountains.

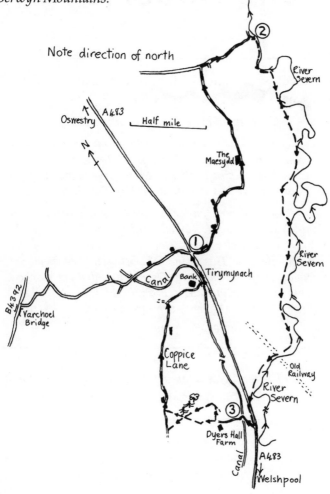

There is a network of footpaths which should make the road walking unnecessary, but unfortunately they exist only on the map. At least it is a quiet little lane, eventually looping back to the A483. Before it does, though, our route turns right at a T-junction with a "No Through Road" sign. Ignore the lane with a second "No Through Road" sign on the right in 100 yards and continue until the lane turns left, with an embankment ahead, which should be climbed.

This is the Tirymynach Embankment, part of the flood defences for the River Severn, which can be seen below. Across the river are the Breidden Hills. [Breidden may mean "walled town on a hill", but I have also seen Craig Breidden translated as Brython's Rock.] The hills were formed from volcanic lava bubbling up through the earth's crust over 400 million years ago, in the Ordovician era (named, aptly perhaps, after a Welsh border tribe). Breidden Hill to the left is made of dolerite and much of it has been quarried and gone through the processing plant at the base of the hill for roadmaking. On top of the hill is a column erected in honour of Admiral Rodney (1719-1792), scourge of the French and Spanish. Further to the right Moel y Golfa [Golfa's Bald Hill] is of andesite. A fabled connection is that Caradoc recruited in the area for troops to fight the Romans. Below the hills is another modern intrusion, the masts of the Criggion [Stony] Radio Station.

2. Turn right along the Offa's Dyke Path, running not along the Dyke, but along the embankment for nearly two miles with numerous solid stiles.

To the left the Severn meanders, sometimes near, at other times spreading out across the alluvial plain, but the embankment is not high enough for its course to be seen completely. The prominent white house halfway to the tree-line on Moel y Golfa is Trewern Cottage.

Soon after a sharp right turn in the embankment the track of an old railway is crossed, and the supports for a bridge over the river can be seen. *The railway once linked Oswestry to Welshpool.* The path leaves the embankment a little further on, level with a

Top Lock, Pool Quay

church, and slants across a field towards the A483 as the River Severn leaves it for the last time. The road is reached by a stile to the right of a prominent gate nearly opposite a farm. Cross the road and turn left along the footpath.

Leave the A483 soon, along a lane which cuts back to the right. The Offa's Dyke Path leaves our route, turning left along the towpath of what was the Montgomeryshire Branch of the Shropshire Union Canal.

This was built in the 1790's, linking with the Llangollen Canal near Ellesmere, but ideas of linking the Severn and the Dee came to nothing. The railway whose bed we have just crossed was a major factor in the decline of the canal, but a section at Welshpool has been reopened and there are plans to extend the renovation. Perhaps the Lottery will help!

3. Our path crosses the canal, with a good view of the last of what was a number of locks coming up from Ardd-lin, and bends left and right as a lane climbing the hill and then dipping down to Dyers Hall Farm. Keep ahead through the farmyard, with a partly wooden building to the right, through a gate directly ahead and then up to where the track turns right. From here there are two possible routes. The farmer would prefer walkers to keep to the track (although it is not a formal right of way). This also gives the better walking. To do this turn right with the stony track and proceed with a hedge to the right. Bear left when another track comes in from the right and then bear left up past a solitary oak tree and between further trees. *Behind there is a fine view of the Breidden Hills and the flood plain of the River Severn.* The track converges with a band of trees to the right, bends right past the end of the trees, crossing a stream, and then goes up to a gate onto Coppice Lane.

If you prefer to stick to the right of way, from the first bend in the track scramble up the bank on the left as soon as possible, and get back to the edge of a wooded dingle. Climb alongside this as far as a ruin on the left. *There are lovely views of the Breiddens across the Severn on this climb.* Bear right here, passing an isolated oak tree to cross a little valley at the left of a line of conifers (as on the other variant). Cross the stream and turn half left here to cross a field diagonally, towards the tree to the left of the largest one in the hedgerow. There is a climbable fence hidden in the hedge over which a lane (Coppice Lane) is reached.

From either the fence or the gate turn right along the lane with a grass strip between tarmac ones.

There are good views from the ridge to both sides (when hedges do not obstruct), with the wooded Gaer-fawr [Great Camp] Hill nearby on the left, with a complicated system of defences hidden in the wood on the top. Much of Montgomeryshire lies behind.

Continue past farm buildings and then descend between higher banks. Pass a pair of cottages which are on the right. At a junction of tracks turn right to climb slightly and then skirt Bank Farm, bending left and right. Go over the canal bridge and go left down to the A483. Turn left along the footway for about 300 yards to return to the start of the walk.

Buttington and Welshpool

An initial climb up to the Beacon Ring Hill Fort, with views into Shropshire as well as over the Severn Valley across Wales, then a choice of routes in the valley, including some through Welshpool.

Distance: *6½ miles without the loop to Welshpool; 8¾ miles via Welshpool and the canal; 9 miles via Welshpool and Gungrog Farm.*

Start: *Begin in* **Buttington** *at the junction of the A458 and the B4388, near the Green Dragon Inn. There is some space for parking on the verge of the B4388 a bit further south. Grid ref: 250 088 (Landranger 126, Pathfinder 888). In* **Welshpool** *there is a large car park at grid ref: 226 076 (Same maps). Join the route description at point 3.*

By bus: *Buttington is on service D75 between Shrewsbury and Llanidloes via Welshpool (Midland Red North, Shrewsbury). Welshpool is also accessible by bus from Oswestry—primarily service D71 (Midland Red North, Oswestry).*

By train: *Welshpool is on the Birmingham—Shrewsbury—Machynlleth—Aberystwyth line. The route passes the station just before point 3.*

Buttington [Archers' Town] was the site of a battle in which King Alfred defeated the Danes. The site of Strata Marcella Abbey (founded in 1170) is nearby. The church is usually open "for prayer and meditation" and has several interesting features, in spite of having been twice restored in the 19th century. The main structure dates from the 14th century. The timberwork, notably the scalloped roof timbers reminiscent of false woodwork on "black-and-white" houses, dates from the 15th century. The glass in the west window is late medieval/Elizabethan. The font has been made from stonework of about 1220/30 from the demolished Strata Marcella Abbey nearby. On the outside the wooden belfry is unusual. The building in the corner of the churchyard was the village school from 1838 to 1953.

The Route

1. Walk along the B4388 past the church. Next pass Buttington House, a square stone building with a brick addition at the rear. Beyond the Offa's Dyke Business Park on the left there is a footway which goes as far as the Offa's Dyke Path (ODP) sign pointing over a stile to the left. The Dyke itself crosses the road at this point and traces can be seen in the field beyond School House as you go up a green lane. Leave this by a stile on the right and head diagonally across the field to another stile to the left of a large oak tree.

The whole of the hilly ridge ahead is referred to as Long Mountain. Geologically it is an example of "inverted relief", which means that the rock is covered by a thick layer of stony clay, giving good farming land even as high as 1300'.

After the stile bear more to the left in the next field to a stile in the corner of the field (just to the left of a power line post). After the stile and a small stone bridge turn left up the field and keep the hedge on the left as you climb. After a stile join a farm track which later bears right to a marker post. Continue on the track to just before the buildings of Stone House Farm. Take the stile on the right and then head to the right of the buildings.

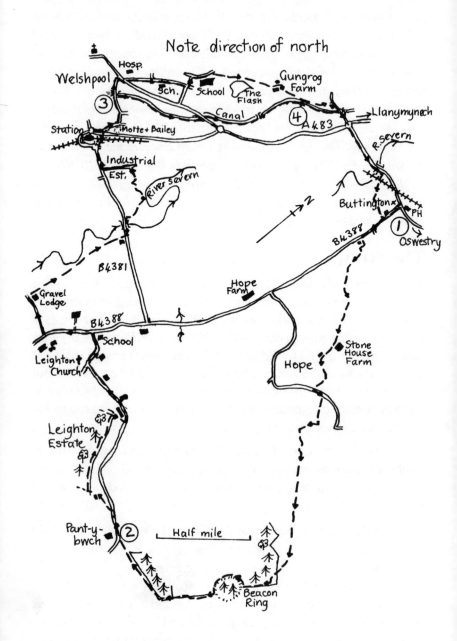

Note direction of north

Take the obvious track, pausing to notice Welshpool below with Powis Castle prominent to the left, below woods. Go through a gate on the track and keep to the left of a partially black and white cottage. Go over a stile on the left and bear right to a gateway. Before this turn left over a stile. The path goes up more steeply now with a hedge on the right (but the view is ample excuse for as many breathers as are necessary). When the hedge ceases continue up the field to a clump of ash and field maple. Bear right here, continuing to slant upwards beyond the trees to a stile into a lane.

The area below is marked Hope on the OS map, so it could be said that those getting to here are "beyond Hope"!

Turn left along the lane to a stile on the right above a steep bank. Go over this and head steeply uphill, with a hedge on the right.

Some of the stiles hereabouts are embellished with a carving of a king's head, rather strangely titled "OFFAR EX" (sic). Looking back Breidden Hill can now be seen to the right in line with the Long Mountain, topped by the Rodney Monument and with the Criggion [Stony] Radio Station at its foot. (See walk 17.) The A483, the Shropshire Union Canal, the railway, the River Severn and the B4388 all pass through the valley below.

Continue upwards past the end of the hedge, later joining a rough track at a stile by a clump of sycamore and holly. The track winds upwards climbing gently. Immediately after a gate across the track turn left to climb more steeply again beside a fence. In the next field ignore the painted arrow on the post and bear right, away from the fence, over the steepest part of the hill, to a stile.

This is the best point for seeing Welshpool, the Severn Valley and (on a good day) much of mid Wales.

The path now climbs more gently, with a fence on the left, through a long field and a short one. In the next field follow a sheep track (with care if you wish to keep your boots clean).

The track slants right towards the top left corner of Cwmdingle Plantation. (This sounds like Anglo-Welsh tautology to me—like the River Avon [River], as Cwm = dingle.) From a marker post the path slants more towards the plantation, which it enters by a stile. The path is well waymarked through the gloomy wood, to run along the south-eastern edge, with some distant views into Shropshire. *The general ambience is not improved by a Severn Trent Water installation with two very obtrusive communication towers.* Just beyond this Beacon Ring Hill Fort is reached.

The fort is early British, and its Welsh name, Caer Digol [Perfect Castle], may relate either to its circular shape or its location. It seems to have been a popular site for battles in the past. The Welsh under Cadwalla fought the Saxons here and in 1295 Madoc, the last Champion of Gwynedd, was beaten and captured by the troops of Edward I. The Welsh could be said to have avenged this soon after, as Owen Tudor, to become Henry VII at Bosworth Field, mustered his adherents from North Wales and Shropshire here. The trees in the middle of the fort were planted as a memorial to Helen Solveig Ackers of Leighton Hall. There is a damaged memorial on the far side. This area is a favourite for butterflies in the summer.

The path is waymarked to the right, round the western fortifications of the fort. *(On a previous visit the paths each way round the rim were prominent, as a result of which I did several trips round before realising that my companions, masked by the trees, had gone on ahead.)* Leave the hill fort by the path to the south, opposite the entry point. In the first field the fence is on the right, but then a stile leads over to the other side. The next stile leads into the fringes of another coniferous wood, Phillips's Gorse. Leaving this by a gate turn right and descend alongside the wood. Over the next stile go ahead down the lane.

2. At Pant-y-bwch [Buck hollow] farm the ODP turns back to the left, but we bear right down the road. When the road narrows, with an almost aerial view of Welshpool ahead, it is possible to continue down it but there is also a pleasant, if rather overgrown, path down the edge of a wood. To reach this follow

Buttington Bridge and the River Severn

the footpath sign on the left over a cattle grid and follow the track round the right hand side of a field. Go over another cattle grid and pass a bungalow (Glenhaven). Just after this, and before a sign welcoming you to the Leighton Estate go through a metal kissing gate on the right of another cattle grid.

The heyday of the estate was in the last century. John Naylor, a banker from Liverpool, had the hall built in 1850-56. Like the Houses of Parliament it was at least partly designed by Pugin, the Neo-gothic architect. Mr Naylor spent £275,000 on the house, gardens and estate. He was a devotee of technology, building a gasworks. His most interesting innovation was to fertilise the local farms through a series of pipes. The fertiliser was held in a huge tank (which may be the fort-like building seen to the left from further down the path). Solid constituents were brought up a funicular railway, and water was driven up from the Severn by a hydraulic ram.

121

Turn right onto the path, which goes down the edge of the wood with a rusty iron fence on the right for a short distance then bears left with a hedge and wooden fence on the right. Keep fairly close to these. There are occasional waymarks for the path. Be particularly careful to follow one which leads ahead rather than turning right through a gate into a field. The path then zigzags left and right in a coniferous section of the wood and eventually reaches a bridleway (with blue waymarks). Turn right here and bend round more to the right to rejoin the road. Turn left and pass a group of houses on the left with stone arch gateways, probably built for workers on the Leighton Estate.

Continue down the road, preferably keeping in single file on the right as the road can be quite busy. Bend right at the entrance to the churchyard. *There may be llamas in the next field on the left!* Two left bends, between houses, bring you down to the B4388, with a school on the right. If you wish to return to Buttington immediately, turn right and continue along the B4388 for about 1¾ miles. (There is a wide verge on the right).

If you wish to go to Welshpool turn left along the footway beside the road. When the tarmacked footway ceases cross the road and continue in the same direction, on the verge when necessary. Pass the entrance to an architectural salvage firm. As the road swings left, with a number of buildings on the left, turn right down the track to Gravel Lodge. The track goes between fences almost straight for about 400 yards, with a stream on the right.

Just before Gravel Lodge the stream passes through an ornamental water meadow with pretty bridges. Turn right with the track, but when it turns again into Gravel Lodge go ahead through a gate. Head towards a pair of power line poles and pass to the right of them, now on an embankment.

Over to the left, to the left of new buildings, Powis Castle is prominent. Soon the River Severn can be seen to the left, still carving away at the farmland on the other bank, and even removing a section of the embankment.

A rustic stile and a gate lead into the next two fields. Keep on the embankment, with a fine avenue of oak trees on the right, and go through another gate to pass another lodge (with a beautifully tended garden) to reach the B4381.

Cross the road and turn left here, crossing the Severn on Leighton Bridge, with a view of the Breidden Hills to the right. Immediately turn back to the right over a stile (before what looks to be a site for travellers). Turn left and keep round the hedge and fence on the left. Soon before reaching a loop of the Severn take a stile on the left and go right over another cattle bridge. Then go with a fence on the left and again take a stile on the left just before the river. Turn left along the fence to reach a track with the metal fence of a sewage works on the right. Follow this fence round to the right and then go left along a road onto an industrial estate. Turn left along the road at a T-junction to meet the B4381 again.

Turn right and go ahead at a mini-roundabout. Go all the way over the footbridge which crosses the railway and the re-routed A483 near Welshpool station. Cross the road and turn right along the footpath past three entrances to the livestock market.

Opposite the third is the site of a 12th century motte and bailey castle, which was the main defence of Welshpool until Powis Castle was built. The site is now occupied by the Victoria Bowling Club, but only the remains of the outer fortifications can be seen.

Bend round left with the road, passing several more entrances to the livestock market, to the canal bridge.

Welshpool received its first market charter in the late 13th century. If you wish to learn more about it you can turn left along the canal to visit the Powysland Museum and Canal Centre, passing the canal wharf opened by the Prince of Wales in 1993. There are also toilets (paying) and an Information Centre at the far end of the main car park a little further on the left.

3. *From this point it is possible to reach Buttington either along the canal or via Gungrog [Meadow of the Cross] Farm. The Gungrog Farm route is initially built-up, passing through a housing estate. The canal also takes some time to reach the country, passing the sheep section of the livestock market and housing estates en route. It is, though, the only opportunity in this set of walks to walk on the 7 mile length of the Montgomeryshire Canal which is all that has been re-opened to traffic.*

Canal route. Go down the steps and turn under the bridge. When you reach the road formerly known as the A483 the canal goes through a small tunnel with no provision for walkers (or barge-pulling horses) so it is necessary to keep to the right of a pool where the vegetation is taking over. Cross the road (thanking your lucky stars that much of the traffic now goes along the new road by the station) to a flight of steps back onto the towpath. The scenery is now more rural (except for yet another new estate across the canal), and you have joined the Severn Way. The next bridge is a proper canal one and leads to Gungrog Farm, which can be seen over to the left. Soon there is a new industrial estate on the right, which will be screened by trees when they have had chance to grow. Turn right just before the next bridge unless you wish to have a look at Buttington Wharf (just beyond it) which has an information board. Join the Gungrog Farm alternative at point 4.

Gungrog Farm route. Pass over the canal. Continue up to the top of the road, turn right along the main road and very soon fork left into Gungrog Road. Pass the entrance to the Victoria Memorial Hospital and then an infants' school. Turn left at a T-junction and bear right on Bronwylfa [Hillside Lookout] Road with a large school on the right. A footpath sign on the right now leads onto a hedged path. Through a kissing gate the path continues with a hedge on the right. When the hedge bends right towards The Flash keep ahead to meet another hedge (not joining it too soon in order to avoid a boggy patch). Continue with this hedge on the right to Gungrog Farm.

Enter the farmyard through a gate and leave it by a flight of steps leading up to a metal gate. Go through the gate and turn right to another gate beside a large sycamore tree. Turn left and angle down towards the canal. Pass through two gateways adjacent to the canal and one further from it. Now bear left to a stile at the left of a house, followed by a gate onto a lane. Turn right along this.

4. As you pass over the canal bridge Long Mountain is ahead of you. Go down to the roundabout and leave it on the opposite road, the A458 to Shrewsbury. This is a busy road with no footway, but the verge on the right is wide enough to be walked along when necessary. You rejoin the Offa's Dyke Path just before crossing the Severn on Buttington Bridge. It is possible to continue along the road to Buttington, crossing the railway at a level crossing.

If you are anxious not to miss out a section of the ODP, turn right over a stile just after the bridge and go down to and across the railway (at a footpath crossing). Head straight across the next field to a stile. Bear left to a footbridge and continue in the same direction to a stile. Bear slightly right to another stile which leads onto the B4388. Turn left to the church and the start of the walk.

Mara Publications

Mara Publications publish a range of walking books for Cheshire and North Wales and have the following list to date

North Wales

Coastal Walks around Anglesey (volume 1)
ISBN 0 9522409 6 3. A collection of 15 walks which explore the varied scenery of Anglesey's beautiful coastline.

Coastal Walks around Anglesey Volume 2
ISBN 0 9522409 5 5. A companion volume to the above book, outlining 15 new walks spread around Anglesey's fascinating and beautiful coastline.

Circular Walks in the Conwy Valley
ISBN 0 9522409 7 1. A collection of 15 circular walks which explore the varied scenery of this beautiful valley from the Great Orme to Betws y Coed.

Walking in the Clwydian Hills and the Vale of Llangollen
ISBN 0 9522409 3 9. A collection of 15 circular walks exploring the beautiful hills and valleys of the Welsh borders.

Walking on the Lleyn Peninsula
ISBN 1 902512 00 6. A collection of 16 circular walks which explore the wild and beautiful coastline and hills of the Lleyn Peninsula.

Cheshire

A Walker's Guide to the Wirral Shore Way
ISBN 0 9522409 0 4. This book describes a linear walk of 23 miles following the old coastline between Chester and Hoylake.

Circular Walks along the Sandstone Trail
ISBN 0 9522409 2 0. The Sandstone Trail is Cheshire's best known and most popular walking route. This book gives a complete

route description along with 12 circular walks covering the entire trail

Circular Walks along the Gritstone Trail and Mow Cop Trail
ISBN 0 9522409 4 7. A route which follows Cheshire's eastern border along the edge of the Peak District. Following the same format as the Sandstone Trail book—a full description for both trails is combined with 12 circular walks.

Circular Walks in Wirral
ISBN 1 902512 02 2. A collection of 15 circular walks in the coast and countryside of Wirral.

Local History

Picturesque Wirral
ISBN 0 9522409 9 8. A reprint of part of T A Coward's "Picturesque Cheshire" dealing with Wirral, originally published in 1903. A fascinating glimpse of Wirral in the closing years of the nineteenth century.

Picturesque Cheshire—Chester and the Welsh border
ISBN 1 902512 03 0. Like the above, this is a reprint of two chapters from T A Coward's "Picturesque Cheshire", originally published in 1903, dealing with the city of Chester and the western limits of the county bordering Wales. A fascinating glimpse of this historic city in the closing years of the nineteenth century.

Forthcoming books:

Walking the Anglesey Coastal Path
ISBN 1 902512 04 9.

Circular walks on the Offa's Dyke Path Volume 2—Welshpool to Hay-on-Wye.